A Sicilian in East Harlem

A SICILIAN
IN EAST HARLEM

Salvatore Mondello

CAMBRIA
PRESS

YOUNGSTOWN, NEW YORK

This book has been registered with the Library of Congress.

Mondello, Salvatore
    A Sicilian in East Harlem / Salvatore Mondello
    p.   cm.
    Includes bibliographical references
    ISBN10 0-9773567-2-8
    ISBN13 978-0-9773567-2-0

To my son Charles with Love

CONTENTS

A Sicilian
in East Harlem

PREFACE

This book is an autobiographical study of Italian Americans in East Harlem, New York in the twentieth century. It emphasizes the Sicilian experience in upper Manhattan.

Italian East Harlem had a brief existence much like boom and bust towns of the Old West. When residents of Italian East Harlem became successful financially, they left the community. Italian East Harlem suffered from a "brain drain" throughout its short history in contrast to Black Harlem, a more stable community. It was challenging for children especially to be growing up in a dying community, one in which families were eager to leave rather than to enter. Ironically, as a child I had the opportunity to leave East Harlem but elected to stay. I am a Sicilian American historian. I tell the story of my Sicilian people and their culture in upper Manhattan as a personal experience. I integrate their story with the stories of other groups and individuals living in East Harlem when it was called Italian East Harlem. Brooklyn and Rochester, New York are a part of my story and they are represented in this book.

I would like to thank Luciano J. Iorizzo, Salvatore LaGumina, Sue Troiano, Pellegrino Nazzaro and Daniel Palermo for reading the manuscript and for their suggestions. A special thanks to Anita Crapanzano, Maria Rampello and Alfred Mondello for their enthusiastic help in finding family sources and recalling family events. Mitchell Mondello found important sources on the life of Saint Benedict and the history of San Fratello. Of course, I alone am responsible for any errors. I should be lacking in gratitude if I failed to acknowledge the professional support of Dr. Paul Richardson and his staff at the Cambria Press. Their belief in my work has made this book possible.

Dr. Salvatore Mondello
Professor Emeritus
Rochester Institute of Technology

FOREWORD

Its geo-political position has made the island of Sicily since ancient times a place of convergence and divergence for many different ethnic groups. Sicily is the largest island of the Mediterranean. Location and size have determined her history and have shaped the character of her inhabitants from prehistoric times to the present.

Many were its settlers and colonizers but all acted as conquerors. They brought to Sicily their lifestyles, traditions, customs and cultures and tried to impose them on the natives. In so doing, they tried to change the identity of the islanders. The conquerors left significant marks but failed to change the character of the Sicilian people.

British historians have made important contributions to our understanding of the Sicilians. In *A History of Sicily*, M. I. Finley provides an excellent chronological excursus of the history of Sicily from prehistoric times to the period of Byzantine rule. Denis Mack Smith supplements it with his two volumes titled *Medieval*

Sicily: 800–1713 and *Modern Sicily: After 1713.*

During Palaeolithic times, immigrants from the Rhone and Spain settled in Sicily. The Neolithic period saw the emergence of the culture in the Syracuse and Catania areas characterized by fortified villages. In the eighth century B.C. the Greeks moved into Sicily and found the island populated by Sicans and Sicels. The Greeks migrated westward for economic reasons. Over time they became settlers and colonizers giving birth to Magna Graecia. Sicels and Greeks differed significantly but lived together in peace until the Greeks tried to subjugate or expel them.

In some areas of Sicily occupied by the Greeks, the Sicels were forced to live in ghettoes or reservations. Other Sicilians, untouched by Hellenization, never lost their identity. Revolts erupted against the Greeks in different parts of the island where the invaders were dominant. One of the most important revolts was led by Ducetius in 450 B.C. in the Syracuse area. Although crushed by the Greek armies, the revolt symbolized the Sicilian willingness to fight foreign oppressors to maintain their identity and culture.

The First Punic War (264–241) brought Rome into Sicily with disastrous consequences for the Carthaginians and the Sicilians alike. Thousands of Sicilians were sold into slavery or compelled to buy their freedom. Roman occupation of Sicily proved vital to the survival of the city of Rome. Sicily was Rome's granary.

Naval bases established in Sicily helped the Romans defeat the Carthaginians in the Second Punic War (218–201). Following the conflict Roman officials were installed permanently in Sicily. Rome's jurisdiction in Sicily was legally imposed with the Lex

Rupilia in 131 B.C.

The Romans adopted in Sicily the same strategy they used in other regions where their colonization activities were introduced. They confiscated properties and land and established the ager publicus, the foundation of the future Sicilian latifundium, a landed estate owned by a powerful man and his family. Sicilians were enslaved on Roman properties and revolts ensued. Charismatic slaves led these uprisings.

Roman domination of Sicily ended when the Byzantine Belisarius captured the island in A.D. 535. The Byzantine occupation left few cultural and social marks on the islanders.

Far more significant was the Arab conquest of the island from 827 to 1091. This occupation brought Sicily into the modern world. A new language, religion and culture were introduced. The Sicilian language assimilated hundreds of Arab words. The Arabs transformed Sicily into a dynamic Middle Eastern culture. The industrial sector flourished and provided an incremental development of the economy. Thousands of Muslims settled in Sicily bringing their sciences, customs and laws to the island. Denis Mack Smith states that the Arab conquest "made Sicily part of a splendid African civilization." However, Sicily became a battlefield for Islam and Christianity. In Sicily the theological arguments among Christians, Muslims, Manichaeans and others remained doctrinaire and therefore irrelevant to the Sicilian people.

The Norman conquest from 1091 until 1200 introduced in Sicily feudalism, eminent domain and baronage. Sicily emerged as a European power and Palermo became a great metropolis.

The next stage in Sicily's history saw it ruled by three powerful royal families: the Hohenstaufen, the Angevines and the Aragones. Frederick II (1197–1250) was a member of the Hohenstaufen family. Educated in Sicily, he possessed an inquisitive mind. He knew many languages. He enjoyed debating with astronomers, mathematicians and philosophers. When he took over the government of Sicily he attempted to eradicate banditry, reduce the power of the barons and restore the central authority. In 1231 the municipalities became dependent on the authority of the emperor. The Inquisition was introduced to crush heretical sects. Frederick II founded the University of Naples in 1224 to educate jurists and administrators. He was stupor mundi.

The Angevines became Sicily's rulers under Charles. A Frenchman, Charles was ambitious and arrogant. Charles of Anjou ordered his armies to confiscate properties which he distributed to French settlers. The brutal rule of the French led to the popular uprising on Easter Sunday of 1282 known as the Sicilian Vespers.

Spain replaced France as the dominant power in Sicily following the revolt of 1282, an occupation lasting until 1713. Under Spanish rule the barons increased their power on the island at the expense of the peasants. A middle class did not emerge. Banditry, piracy and the constant bribery of public officials were the unfortunate consequences of arbitrary baronial rule. Banditry led to the rise of the capi popolo, mob leaders in opposition to the barons. Shady characters were idolized as defenders of the oppressed.

The Treaty of Utrecht of 1713 assigned Sicily to Victor Amedeus, Duke of Savoy. He could not adjust himself to the extravagance of the barons and remained unpopular with them. In 1720 the Habsburgs of Austria obtained control of Sicily but lost the island to Spain. Spanish rule lasted until Garibaldi and the Red Shirts arrived in Marsala in 1860. The plebiscite of October 1860 ended the insularity of Sicily and led to its annexation to Piedmont. Later, it became a part of the Kingdom of Italy under Victor Emanuel II. Sicily had come full circle. After centuries of foreign occupations and colonizations, Sicily ended up with perhaps an inevitable Italian identity politically and administratively.

Giuseppe di Lampedusa writes in his masterpiece *The Leopard* that Sicilians maintain "una insularità d'animo," an insularity of the soul wherever they go and live.

It is against this historical backdrop that Professor Salvatore Mondello's variegated and multi-thematic book should be read and understood. The work underscores that time and distance are irrelevant in remembering and recreating a Sicilian experience. Sicilian traditions, culture and mentality are timeless and Sicilian "insularity" is transmitted generation after generation and remains an ongoing process. Professor Mondello, a Sicilian American born and raised in New York City, discovered his "sicilianità" in an American city far from Sicily. His family's traditions were permeated by a "sicilianità" that preserved the spirit, lifestyle, character and culture of the Mediterranean island.

The most revealing aspects of Mondello's work are the uncompromising principles upon which the Sicilian character is built: family, respect, honor, hard work, steadfast condemnation of abuse, corruption and arrogance and a firm belief in the ultimate success of human ability.

Finally, Mondello's book reveals the spirit of Augustinian historicism based on memory and expectations permeated with classical Sicilian Verismo.

Pellegrino Nazzaro

Professor of History

Rochester Institute of Technology

PART I

A GALLERY
OF URBAN LANDSCAPES

THE FAMILY

It was ten in the evening and I could see him down the block. I watched him as he made his way to the stoop of our building. He was now out of sight. I left the window and went into the kitchen where Grandma Rosalia was warming his minestra. I waited near the big door listening for his cough. I began to hear his heavy breathing as he climbed the few remaining stairs leading to our apartment on the fourth floor. I opened the door and kissed his stubbled cheek. He was home and I felt safe under his paternal protection and affection.

My grandparents and I lived in Italian East Harlem in New York City in the early twentieth century. My maternal grandmother, Rosalia Cassara, was born on April 28, 1890, in San Fratello, Sicily and died in Hempstead, New York, on July 27, 1972. San Fratello is a small village in the Nebrodi Mountains in the Province of Messina and is known for the breeding of Arabian horses introduced in the village during the Muslim occupation of Sicily. She and I spent most of our time in East Harlem. Her San Fratellese dialect was the language of some Sicilian poets.

My grandfather, Alfio Cassara, was born in San Fratello, Sicily, on January 5, 1883, the son of Cirino Cassara and his wife Rosalia Mondello. Alfio did not participate in the life of One Hundred and Seventh Street, our block in East Harlem between First and Second avenues. Alfio was told to come to East Harlem by a shoemaker from San Fratello who had a shoe repair shop on One Hundred and Seventh Street and needed another shoemaker. Alfio worked for him until he had enough money set aside to open his own shoe repair and hat cleaning shop with his nephew Charles on Columbus Avenue. From that time on Alfio saw East Harlem only in the mornings when he left for work and in the evenings when he returned home.

Alfio was Rosalia's uncle as well as her husband. He was seven years her senior. She was illiterate and proud of his ability to read and write in Italian, a language Alfio rarely spoke at home. Alfio had attended school in San Fratello, had learned the shoemaker trade, and had served as a finanziere, a customs officer, before marrying Rosalia, the daughter of Marianna, one of his two sisters. My grandmother was sixteen when she married my grandfather. My grandmother never knew who her father was. All she knew was that her last name was Coppa. Alfio was the youngest of five children.

To save his family from poverty, Alfio decided to emigrate to New York City in 1906. An immigration inspector at Ellis Island placed a chalk mark on Alfio's jacket believing he had an eye infection. Alfio brushed the chalk mark away and landed in New York. There is no official record at Ellis Island of his coming to

America. In the first fifteen years of the twentieth century approximately 3.5 million Italians came to the United States. The major causes of emigration out of Italy included growth in population, capitalist innovations that disrupted traditional farming and craft production, heavy taxes and military conscription. Sicilians in my neighborhood liked to say "la miseria" forced them out of Italy.

South Italian shoemakers migrated in large numbers in the early twentieth century to France, Switzerland, Algeria, Tunisia, Brazil, Argentina and the United States. They settled in urban areas. Traditional village craftsmen persisted in the Italian South in the first decades of the twentieth century. My grandfather made boots and shoes but in New York he made his living primarily repairing shoes. Rich Jewish customers from Central Park West, however, continued to order his handmade boots.

Alfio settled in Italian East Harlem. The first Italians to arrive in East Harlem were strikebreakers hired by an Irish contractor to build the trolley tracks along First Avenue. They came sometime in the 1870's. An Italian workers' shantytown emerged along the East River and One Hundred and Sixth Street in an area called Jones Woods. Soon Italian immigrants from the Mulberry Street area in lower Manhattan flooded the East Harlem area. They came looking for jobs in construction and the rapid transit lines. They found apartments in East Harlem because it was a cleaner and healthier community than the slum of lower Manhattan. From the 1920's to World War II only the area from One Hundred and Fourth to One Hundred and Nineteenth streets between Third Avenue and the East River was predominantly Italian. Italians moved into tenements with or near Irish, German and Jewish residents. Most of the Italians came from southern Italy. In streets where the majority of residents were Italians, neighborhood loyalties were strong. Housing was substandard in Italian East Harlem. In the 1930's Italian women marched for better housing and cleaner streets. By 1930 East Harlem housed eighty-nine thousand Italians of the first and second generations. East Harlem stretched from Ninety-Sixth Street to One Hundred and Twenty-Fifth Street and from Lexington Avenue to the East River.

The New York City Department of Health conducted a study comparing the health of Italians living in lower Manhattan and East Harlem with their contiguous non-Italian sections for the years from 1929 to 1931. In lower Manhattan the Italians had higher percentages of tuberculosis and pneumonia cases than the contiguous non-Italian neighborhood. In East Harlem the Italians had a lower percentage of tuberculosis cases than their contiguous non-Italian community and only a slightly higher percentage of pneumonia cases. Cancer cases were very low in Italian East Harlem compared with the contiguous community and with the Italians in lower Manhattan. The East Harlem Health Center had been in existence for more than a decade and the authors of the study attributed the good results in the East Harlem community to its work.

Italian unskilled laborers were an embattled group in East Harlem in the early years of the twentieth century. The New York subway was built primarily by Italian immigrant workers. They were not members of unions and were exploited by contractors. Early in 1903 Tito Pacelli of the Masons' Union and Herman

Robinson of the American Federation of Labor founded the Rock-men's Union and the Excavators' Union. Hundreds of Italians joined and many more were sympathetic to the goals of the unions. On May 1, 1903, a strike was called by the unions demanding higher wages. At first, the Italians refused to accept a settlement giving them less than was originally demanded. Violence erupted. Each morning Italian strikers appeared near the excavations and attacked strikebreakers with stones and knives. A group of Italian strikers and their wives assaulted Irish workers laying track on Third Avenue. The Italians finally settled for a smaller increase in wages than they had demanded. The Rockmen's and Excavators' unions didn't survive the Depression of 1907, when many Italians returned to Italy. But the 1903 strike proved to union leaders that Italian unskilled workers could be organized.[1] Years later, I attended an exhibit of mosaics Sicilian artisans had created for some of the New York subway stations. Mosaics were introduced in Sicily by the Arabs during their occupation of the island. The exhibit was held at the Brooklyn Museum of Art.

The South Italians were not welcomed with open arms by American journalists during the mass migration to the United States. For example, in The World's Work a writer deplored in 1914 the tremendous influx of South Italians in America. The United States did not attract many North Italians, whose "brains and ability" made Italy a progressive country, the author asserted. Instead, America received "the undersized, illiterate overflow from half-medieval Naples and Sicily." This commentator called for a discriminatory law against the admission of South Italians, similar to the legislation excluding Chinese. Articles such as this one deploring the South Italian migration to America were the rule rather than the exception from the 1880's through the 1920's. In a letter dated June 2, 1860 from Palermo, Henry Adams remarked that the Sicilians were the "most brutal and savage crowd known in modern Europe."[2]

Having established himself in his shop and his tenement apartment on One Hundred and Seventh Street, in 1907 Alfio sent for Rosalia and Marianna as well as his other sister Betty and Betty's children Charles and Angelina. Within a short period of time, Charles got married and went to live in Pelham Bay. Angelina got married, too, and Betty joined her and her husband in the Bronx. Soon, Alfio's brothers, Giuseppe and Luigi, came to America looking for economic opportunities. Giuseppe was lazy and Luigi had a drinking problem. They worked for about five years in construction but they were often unemployed and decided to return to San Fratello. Luigi had left his wife in San Fratello and had not seen her during his stay in New York. Giuseppe's daughters, Mary and Fanny, lived for six years with Alfio, Rosalia and Marianna, but they were unhappy in East Harlem and returned to Sicily. Charles Whibley, an English literary critic and journalist, visited New York City in the same year my grandmother came to East Harlem. He considered New York City a "magic cauldron," and the immigrants "who are cast into it are born again."[3]

By marrying Rosalia and bringing her to America, Alfio had saved her from the grinding poverty that destroyed the lives of so many Sicilians following the unification of Italy. Italy had no common language, no common culture, and many South Italians considered themselves conquered by the armies and politicians of the northern regions. It appeared to the South Italians that the Mezzogiorno, the Italian South, had become a colony of the North Italians. The old Bourbon rulers had been replaced by the Piedmontese and the Lombards. Giovanni Verga makes Sicilian poverty the subject of many of his short stories. In "Nedda" published in 1874 Verga tells the tragic story of a young woman who works for low wages in the olive groves and elsewhere to support herself and her dying mother. She fell in love with Janu but he died before they could get married. Her infant daughter dies and Nedda thanks the Virgin Mary for taking her from the earth "so that she wouldn't have to suffer like me."[4] In Verga's "Rosso Malpelo," appearing in 1878, a young man works like a beast of burden in a quarry and dies there. The young man rarely saw the sky.[5]

Alfio and Rosalia had a son, Charles, who died from meningitis when he was only a year and a half, and a daughter, Rosalie. She was born on October 12, 1911. Marianna loved Rosalie and spoiled her. She bought her many dresses until Rosalia complained. Alfio spoiled her, too. On Sundays he took her to South Beach and Coney Island where they enjoyed eating clam chowder. My grandmother worked in a nearby shirt factory in those early years and devoted little time to her daughter. Rosalia was a pretty young woman and a photographer took a picture of her working at her sewing machine. The other women were upset since the photographer didn't take pictures of them. Rosalie started elementary school with no knowledge of English or Italian. She spoke only the San Fratellese dialect. When a teacher punished Rosalie by hitting her on the hands with a ruler, Marianna went to the school and shook the teacher violently until she swore never to hit her granddaughter again. Rosalie finished her public schooling at the age of fourteen. She spent the next four years studying dress designing at a private school on Twenty-eighth Street and Fifth Avenue run by Antoinette Zingali Grandi. One of the students was Edith Head who became a famous Hollywood dress designer. Rosalie remembered Edith as "quick in learning and bright." Each student made her own gown for graduation. Madame Grandi told Rosalie to open her own dress shop. However, Rosalie worked only one day in a nearby shirt factory. She complained that her fingers hurt her and Alfio told her to stay at home. He bought her a piano but she stopped playing it after several lessons. Piano rolls came with the piano and these were enjoyed by the entire family. She took mandolin lessons and enjoyed playing that instrument.

Alfio Cassara read *Il Progresso Italo-Americano*, the largest and oldest Italian-language daily newspaper in the United States, bought for more than two million dollars by Generoso Pope. On April 1, 1891 Generoso Pope was born in Pasquarielli, Italy, a town near Benevento. He emigrated to New York City in May 1906. At first he worked as an unskilled laborer. Jobs were plentiful for immigrants in New York City. Subway construction began in 1900. The Manhattan and Queensborough bridges were completed by 1909. Steel made possible the building of skyscrapers, including the Flatiron Building in 1902. By 1914 he was superintendent of the Colonial Sand and Stone Company. By 1918 he and Lawrence Rukeyser bought Colonial from the original owners and by 1926 they controlled most of the sand dealerships in the city. In the following year Pope forced Rukeyser out of all their businesses. Active in politics and the unions, Pope supplied the sand and concrete for the new airports, Radio City, Rockefeller Center, and municipal housing projects. By 1932 Pope owned three Italian-language newspapers in New York City, including *Il Progresso* and an Italian daily in Philadelphia. He remained, like my grandfather and other Italian immigrants, a staunch supporter of the Italian dictator Benito Mussolini until the Fascist dictator joined forces with Germany and Japan in World War II. Pope rehabilitated himself with President Roosevelt by his active participation in the war effort. My grandfather's news came from *Il Progresso* and he reported the news to my grandmother and me when I was a child. During the war grandpa lost all of the savings he had deposited in Italian banks. He cursed Mussolini "for stealing my money."[6]

My mother had men who dated her. She didn't like any of them including a gangster, finding them "too good." Apparently, they were gentlemen. She preferred a suitor with rough edges and fell in love with her distant cousin Benedict Mondello. He was a more "demanding" man than her other dates. Benedict and Rosalie were married in 1930 against the wishes of her parents. Benedict was the second child of Paula and Salvatore Mondello. Benedict had four brothers and an older sister, Rose, who was married to a notorious gangster. Paula died early in life. She was rushed to the hospital where an appendectomy was performed. In the recovery ward, she was given water to drink and this mistake led to her death. While my paternal grandfather was working shoveling coal for Con Edison, his children were roaming the streets of East Harlem unattended by any adult. Public authorities stepped in and the children were placed in the Mount Loretto Orphanage in Staten Island. Salvatore was told that he could reclaim his children if he could provide adult supervision for them.

A man named Visconti from San Fratello owned a creamery in Stockertown, Pennsylvania and three retail Italian cheese stores in New York City and wished to sell his entire business. Salvatore, his brothers Charles and Al, and his brother-in-law Rosario, pooled their resources and purchased the creamery and the stores. Salvatore went to work in the creamery taking his children with him while each of his partners ran the stores in Bayridge, Brooklyn, One Hundred and Twenty-first Street in East Harlem, and Arthur Avenue in the Bronx. When Rose and her husband died, Rose's brother Fred took care of their three sons, sharing his apartment with them on One Hundred and Sixth Street. Later, Salvatore took care of them in his apartment in the Bronx.

The creamery was a large stone structure with the factory on the first floor and ten rooms above it. The coal-burning stove didn't always work and in the winter the children slept with their clothes on. The boilers used to transform milk into curd provided some heat during working hours. The children went to school, worked in the creamery after school, and occasionally helped local farmers with their chores. When they grew older, they worked in the stores. Unlike Alfio Cassara, Salvatore Mondello had friends. He had a drinking buddy, a plumber, and he liked to go to a local bar where he drank and talked with a female companion. His mother, Pauline, lived for more than one hundred years and was cared for by Salvatore's sister Angelina and her husband Rosario who owned a brownstone property in Brooklyn.

Salvatore Mondello outlived all of his partners and by the 1950's was the sole owner of the Stockertown Cheese Company, which included the creamery and the only remaining store on Arthur Avenue. Now in his seventies a woman from his village of San Fratello asked him to marry her. Salvatore rejected her offer of marriage believing that marriage was a once in a lifetime affair. Salvatore eventually brought all of his sons into the thriving business. My brother Alfred worked for Salvatore, too. Alfred noted that Salvatore respected his customers and made superior Italian cheeses. His customers came from all parts of the country and racketeers from East Harlem liked to shop there. My paternal grandfather rose from humble beginnings to become a successful businessman in the Italian American community. The success of the early Italian immigrants in East Harlem is the main theme in Garibaldi M. Lapolla's 1935 novel *The Grand Gennaro*, the protagonist using whatever means are necessary to get to the top of the rags and metals businesses in Italian East Harlem.

Sammy Rinaldi, a former resident of One Hundred and Seventh Street, bought his cheeses at the Arthur Avenue store. He shopped for Frank Sinatra and sent the singer his favorite Mondello cheeses by plane. Following Salvatore's death, his sons increased their stealing from one another and eventually the business folded. In the mid-twentieth century, however, the Stockertown Cheese Company store on Arthur Avenue was a Mecca for Italian cheese lovers throughout the United States.

I was born to Rosalie and Benedict Mondello on February 27, 1932, the first of four sons (Alfred, Charles and Benedict). I was baptized at St. Ann's Church at 312 East One Hundred and Tenth Street on May 8, 1932. I was born with blue eyes. Since no other Mondello ever had blue eyes Salvatore Mondello, for whom I was named, insisted I was not his son's child. Twenty-two days after my birth, Benedict abandoned Rosalie and went to live with a Puerto Rican woman. My mother left her new apartment in the Bronx and returned to her parents' apartment on One Hundred and Seventh Street. My grandmother, recently retired from the shirt factory, took care of me since my mother was in a state of depression. I was vaccinated on December 14, 1935. When my grandmother and my mother took me on the bus to the hospital to have my tonsils removed, I discovered that a button was missing from my jacket and asked them to take me home to put a new one on. My request was denied, of course. I stayed in a ward for one night and felt very uncomfortable there.

I remember the dead body of my great-grandmother in a coffin in the middle of our parlor. I saw women screaming hysterically by the coffin. There were no funeral homes in our neighborhood. I never saw my great-grandmother alive.

My father came down with rheumatic fever and returned to my mother. About a year and a half after I was born, Rosalie and

Benedict had their second child, Alfred. When my father's health was restored, my grandfather bought him a quality suit and hat. Alfio gave Benedict money to put a down payment on a truck and to open a small grocery store with Benedict's brother Joseph in Corona, New York. Several months after the store was opened Joseph stole the truck full of merchandise and sold it in Pennsylvania. After this disaster Benedict opened a small grocery store, where credit was given to customers, on Knickerbocker Avenue in Brooklyn. His cousin Charles came in as a partner. When my parents rented an apartment above the store, they moved there taking my brother with them. I refused to go. I cried every day. My grandfather was attached to me and my grandmother convinced her daughter to let me stay at One Hundred and Seventh Street for a few months. I remained with my grandparents until I turned eighteen. When I was eleven my parents came to take me away from my grandparents. A few days later I left Brooklyn to return home, using the subway and the Third Avenue El to effect my escape. I got off the El at the One Hundred and Sixth Street station and ran all the way home. My parents made no further attempts to fetch me. As a child I considered the Third Avenue Elevated Line my road to freedom from my mother and father.

Alfio Cassara was short, obese, bald, and had rough, callused hands from years of cutting leather, but to me he was a hero like Garibaldi. He never lost his teeth. As a child he had picked up a chair with his teeth. My grandfather didn't need friends. He was devoted to me and Rosalia. Grandpa took me out every Sunday to the Bronx Zoo or to amusement parks. We liked Coney Island and

Palisades Park. We enjoyed the World's Fair of 1939 where I got my first glimpse of Mayor Fiorello LaGuardia on the shoulders of my grandfather. On occasion grandpa would take me to the New York Aquarium. On one of those trips he bought me a book on the subject of changing colors among fish. It was published in 1930. It was a book I liked to look at. I still have it in my private library. (The first book that I bought from an elementary school classmate was titled *A Child's Book of Wild Animals*.) Grandma stayed home and prepared meals for us when we returned from our outings. Grandpa promised to take me to Italy when he retired from work, telling me how beautiful Sicily was for those with money. He bought two houses in San Fratello in 1924 and allowed his brother Giuseppe and Giuseppe's son Luigi to live in these properties rent-free. Years later, Alfio managed to sell the house in which Luigi had lived. However, Giuseppe sold Alfio's house to his daughter Carmelina Cassara who later sold it to Sarafina LaMarca for eight million lire. Grandpa never became an American citizen and never returned to Italy but he and I had enchanting moments imagining what it would be like to live in such an earthly paradise.

I got my education in practicality and moral values from my grandmother. Rosalia was frugal in money matters and conservative in her moral teachings. Every Easter period we went to Grossman's clothing store to buy my Easter suits. She would bargain fiercely with Mr. Grossman.

"Come on, Sammy," she would say to me pulling me closer to the door until Mr. Grossman lowered the price to grandma's satisfaction. She made sure that most of my allowance was saved in

Postal Savings for my college education. Italians didn't trust putting their money in banks during the Great Depression. I had to bring glory to my grandparents, she would say. She told me to marry a nice Italian girl. Rosalia knew a woman who lived in sin with her son. She could spot her half a block away and would order me to cross the street to avoid contact with this evil woman. Since Rosalia's son and daughter were brought up by her mother, I was the only child she could rear on her own and she enjoyed every minute of it. Once she had taught me all she knew, she reached the conclusion that I could do nothing wrong. With my clarinet I would play all of her favorite Italian songs including "Mama," and she would praise me after each private performance. Grandma wanted me to enjoy books and took me to the library regularly. I liked the smell of books at the library, a prerequisite for a future recipient of a Ph.D. in history. As I grew older I became her closest friend and she would sit with me for hours telling me Sicilian stories, telling me her problems, telling me her aspirations. No one else, not even grandpa, was made so aware of her inner personality. She liked to tell me that I was a good listener. My relationship with my grandma defies categorization. Perhaps only another Sicilian grandson can understand such a relationship. There were no walls separating me from my grandmother.

Grandma enjoyed the company of the other women in her building. They enjoyed playing the numbers and had a bookie that took their bets once a week. Gossip was a favorite pastime. Their humor was frequently vulgar.

Once each year, on September 17th, Rosalia was given public

recognition by a cymbals player in a marching band. That was the day our street became an Italian piazza with arches of colored lights creating evening rainbows. St. Benedict, a black man, was our patron saint and we honored him every year on that day. When the men who carried the saint stopped in front of our building, Rosalia would throw down a dollar or two wrapped in heavy cord to be pinned to the saint's vestments. The cymbals player was the bandmaster and a man Rosalia had known in her youth in San Fratello. He would raise his cymbals to her in a protracted salute and then removing one of his cymbals he would tip his hat. A big smile from Rosalia from her fourth-story window was his reward.

STREET LIFE

On cool spring mornings I would open my parlor window facing the street and smell the East River. To get to the river I would have to pass One Hundred and Seventh Street between First Avenue and East River Drive. That street had horse and wagon stables. They always smelled of horse manure. When I read my picture books with horses and farms I knew what smell enveloped them. I liked to look at the island on the other side of the pier. Tugboats passed. I wondered how far they could travel? How long would it take to travel from the East River to San Fratello in Sicily where grandpa would buy me a pony and an orchard? Did Italian ponies smell like the horses I passed to get to the pier? I would have to ask my grandpa.

Years later, I learned that one of the stables I passed so frequently to get to the pier had been owned in the early years of the twentieth century by a notorious woman, Pasquarella Spinelli. She employed at the stable a blacksmith, a wheelwright and thugs who stole horses from merchants unwilling to pay Spinelli protection money. She leased tenements in East Harlem and managed the Rex

Theater on Second Avenue. In 1912 she was shot to death by her competitors in the protection racket. During the forties three of the stables near the East River were occupied by milk-bottling companies.

When I was a child grandma was my companion. And my best teacher. Often she used Sicilian proverbs to teach me lessons she considered important for me to know. On the subject of old age she recited, "Lu pisu di l'anni è lu pisu cchiù granni." (The weight of advancing years is the heaviest weight.) On God she noted, "Ogni beni di Diu veni." (Every gift comes from God.) However, she was critical of monks and priests: "Nun aviri cunti cu monaci e parrini." (Have nothing to do with monks and priests.) And one proverb she recited on numerous occasions to me when I was little: "Cui cerca, trova; cui secuta, vinci." (One who searches, finds; one that perseveres, wins.)

Sicilian women had a proverb for shopping: "Cu' accatta abbisogna di cent'occhi; cu' venni d'un sulu." (The shopper needs one hundred eyes, the seller needs only one.)[7]

The young men living on my street were construction workers or merchants. The young women worked in neighborhood factories, many in a shirt-making factory on First Avenue. The grandmothers watched the grandchildren and did the grocery shopping. My great-grandmother shopped with my mother by her side. My grandmother shopped with me by her side.

An American writer, Caroline Singer, shopping on the East Side in 1921 sheds light on the shopping experiences of women like my great-grandmother with my mother at her side. In her Saturday visit Singer noted that every minute spent in the market by the Italians was "pervaded with festive anticipation of the next day's idleness," with its visit to Coney Island or its "platter of ravioli furnishing the major theme for a family reunion." Pleasant aromas pervaded the marketplace. After the baker opened the doors of the ovens in his shop, "the warm odor of golden crusts" seemed to float into the street. The "spicy" fragrances of cakes dotted with caraway delighted her senses. As the mint vendor passed by her, the air grew "unbelievably sweet with perfume from the crushed leaves" he carried in his "bouquet." Everywhere was an abundance of provisions. As the organ grinder moved down the street, he was screened by "mounds of tomatoes and green peppers, with only the top of his dusty hat visible from the sidewalk."[8]

A symphony of smells and sights greeted me every Monday morning when I went shopping with grandma along First Avenue going uptown. On occasion we would stop at Frank Passaro's book and music store at 2091 First Avenue between One Hundred and Seventh and One Hundred and Eighth streets.

"I would like the record 'Mamma' sung by Stefano Lombardi," she asked Mr. Passaro.

"I think I have two records left of that wonderful song," Mr. Passaro replied. "Just a minute Signora Cassara."

I liked to look at his books. Grandma had told me never to touch the books but getting close to them was allowable. There was a golden soldier on the cover of one of the books and I liked the way the soldier was dressed for battle.

Mr. Passaro brought back the 78 and handed it to grandma. He saw me looking at the book.

"That my boy is a copy of Alessandro Dumas, *I Tre Moschettieri*," he told me. "When you learn Italian in school, you may wish to buy it."

"He will learn Italian in school and he will then buy the book," grandma replied.

"Mamma" is the song of an immigrant who wants to see his mother and never again wants to leave her. She represents life itself. Grandma played it so often on the Victrola that when I learned how to play the clarinet I had no difficulty playing the tune from memory. Like many other Italian women of her generation, she enjoyed the singing of Carlo Buti. She liked to hear his singing of such tunes as "Menestrello Vagabondo" and "Stella Alpina." I preferred Bing Crosby, Perry Como and Frank Sinatra. I also liked the singing of Al Jolson.

At the corner of First Avenue and One Hundred and Eighth Street there were two vendors of treats. One old man sold roasted chestnuts. The other man had a yellow and red pushcart and sold roasted franks. Grandma liked the chestnuts and I liked the franks. Eating these treats delayed our grocery shopping but they were worth the delay. Sometimes she would take out her handkerchief to wipe the mustard off my face. "Come on, my son."

Small stores lined the side of the street with buildings and merchants with horse drawn wagons lined the curb. Some merchants sold clothing but most sold food. Grandma had her vinyl bag and her pocketbook and was prepared to make her purchases.

Sometimes we would visit Mr. Nicola at his cappuzzelle store.

He sold sweet meats and this food was popular with Sicilians.

"Buon giorno, Signora Cassara. How is Signore Alfio."

"As well as can be expected of a man who supports his family."

She would look carefully at his displays to determine what came in today and what came in yesterday. Sometimes she would buy tripe. Other times it was liver. The lambs' heads were a special treat but I didn't like eating the eyes. Occasionally she would buy brains. I liked it when she made tripe in her special homemade tomato sauce.

"I'll take a pound and a half of the tripe." She was proud of the way she cleaned tripe. We never got sick eating it.

I liked the smell of Mr. Nicola's store. It had a clean smell. The tiles on the floor were shiny white. His white apron was spotless. His wife must have a scrub board just like grandma and a bathtub to wash his clothes.

We went to the Italian fresh cheese store located near the cappuzzelle store. I didn't like the smell of milk but I did enjoy the taste of mozzarella especially the kind that was smoked. Mozzarella came in braids as well as round with a puckered kiss at the top. The smoked variety was hanging on hooks. The plain mozzarellas were in refrigerators. Ricotta was for sale as well as fresh cheeses in baskets. Grandma bought a plain mozzarella used to make her thick Sicilian pizzas. Sometimes she melted mozzarella over eggplant.

She always bought fruits and vegetables. Grandma made a salad of oranges with olive oil that I liked very much. We never bought bread because grandma made her own. She ordered red wine from a wine merchant who delivered the bottles to our house. Grandma bought provolone and dried sausages in the small grocery store.

Easter was my favorite holiday. I got new clothes for Easter. Grandma bought her only new dress for the year at Easter. Grandma made pignolata for the holiday and I would help her. She beat eggs into the sugar, gradually adding milk and olive oil. Flour came next. We would then make long round sticks. These would be cut into bite-sized nuggets. After these were tossed in boiling oil and golden brown they would be mixed in honey and sprinkled with cinnamon. I still associate the smell of cinnamon with Easter.

The pastry store was located on the corner of First Avenue and One Hundred and Seventh Street. During the Easter season, the baker became a great artist. He made marzipan white lambs on green bases. Sometimes he made a mamma and two or three little ones. To prove that they were American lambs he stuck American flags on toothpicks in the back of each mamma lamb. At a time when Italy was at war with us, it was prudent for the baker to show his patriotism in this unique manner. Years later, Italian American pastry shops found their poet in my friend Rose Basile Green:

Pastry Shops

Let us give praises to embellished bread
By beauty lifted from the sod and cane;
Gross hunger by plain wheat is eased and fed
But barely can the artist's taste sustain.
The flower exudes its perfume from the bower
And makes a garden where the grasses grow;

The magic of creative hands turns flour
Into the pasticcieri that we know.
Sfigliatelle, cannelloni, rum-soaked cakes
With stirring scents of amaretti strain
Their clam and cannon forms tradition makes,
And crowns with pine nuts and confetti grain.
The pastry must not be too sweet, nor over-rich the creams;
So must appear the face of life, not lesser than it seems.[9]

Grandma shopped on Second Avenue too. There were only stores there, no horses and wagons with goods. Her butcher was a relative. She liked the way he cut and pounded her veal cutlets. She made delicious spittini, veal rolls stuffed with salami, cheeses and spices.

The only large grocery store in our neighborhood was located on Second Avenue. She bought her canned and boxed goods there. The proprietor was Jewish. He delivered to our apartment.

Sometimes she made pasta at home and sometimes she bought pasta at the pasta store. The store had a big window with curtains of stringy pasta dangling on hooks. There was an awning over the pasta curtain. I imagined the awning as a cap and the pasta as a skirt. Perhaps the cap and skirt belonged to a giant hoola dancer like the girl I had seen in one of my picture books.

There was a bakery I liked on Second Avenue between One Hundred and Fifth and Sixth streets. It was a sugary paradise, an oasis of sugary treats. On warm and hot days grandma and I would stop there to eat our Italian ices. Sometimes we would order

Italian ice cream.

On very rare occasions grandma and I would shop on the West Side where only Jewish merchants sold goods. There for some reason grandma would bargain with the merchants. She didn't do this with Italian merchants on First and Second avenues.

There were no restaurants in my neighborhood. My grandparents and I ate at home. I was introduced to cafeteria food when I went to James Otis Junior High School and Benjamin Franklin High. This food no matter what it was smelled the same. It was cafeteria-smelling food in the shape and look of hamburgers, mashed potatoes, peas and pasta.

I didn't see my grandpa's shoe repair shop as a child. It was in some faraway place named after Columbus but once a month I smelled leather in the small shoe repair shop on our street. We went there because the shoemaker was the treasurer of the St. Benedict Society of which grandpa was a member. The society paid death benefits to families of deceased members. The shoemaker had a long beard and put nails in his mouth before nailing them to shoes.

I liked the look and smell of burning candles in St. Ann's Church on One Hundred and Tenth Street. Grandpa didn't care for priests and never went to church. Grandma went on those occasions when she needed help from the Virgin Mary or St. Benedict. We would light candles in little glass cups and kneel before Mary. We would cross ourselves with holy water from a fountain upon entering and leaving the church. My grandparents insisted that I make my communion and confirmation. I fell in love with my pretty nun. My grandma feared Protestants and avoided them when possible. She

never walked near the Presbyterian church Norman Thomas established on One Hundred and Sixth Street.

In the middle of September for three days and nights we celebrated the feast of our patron saint, Benedict. Vendors set up their
stalls. Music from the jukebox in the poolroom sounded louder
than ever. The vendors I liked the best roasted peppers and
sausages and boiled corn on the cob. My grandparents never ate
corn; they considered it pigs' food. This was my only opportunity
to eat it. I could smell the roasting peppers and sausages blocks
away. The residents of One Hundred and Seventh Street enjoyed
one big cookout once a year. To me saints, sausages and corn on
the cob would be linked in my memory forever.

September 17, 1946 was a memorable St. Benedict feast day on
our block. Tami Mauriello, the heavyweight boxing contender,
came to see his sister and secure the blessings of St. Benedict in his
fight for the title against Joe Louis the following evening at
Madison Square Garden. Alfred and I believed that Tami could
defeat Louis. Tami had won bouts against tough opponents including Gus Lesnevich, Lee Oma and Jimmy Bivins. Well-wishers
crowded around Tami and his sister expressing their support. The
fight lasted only one round. Tami dazzed Louis but the champion
quickly recovered and finished Tami off. Years later, Tami played
the role of Tullio in "On the Waterfront," a film starring Marlon
Brando.

The annual procession in July honoring Our Lady of Mount
Carmel stopped on each street in East Harlem as suppliants
including my grandmother pinned dollar bills on the robes of the

Madonna. The votive offering varied according to the favor requested of the Madonna. Many women, fingering rosary beads or carrying large candles, marched barefoot in the parade behind the politicians, businessmen, and musicians. My brother Alfred decided to participate in one of these marches. He noticed that a woman we called the "Witch" was marching in the procession. He asked her not to march since he knew she was a witch. At night at One Hundred and Fifteenth Street where Our Lady of Mount Carmel Church was located and in neighboring streets the sights and smells of fried sausages and peppers and fireworks filled the air and titillated the palate as some celebrants danced to tarantellas in Thomas Jefferson Park. This was a feast celebrated by all residents in East Harlem including non-Italians. But the residents of my street enjoyed the feast honoring St. Benedict more because it was our own private feast, honoring a saint whose statue was in one of our stores. St. Benedict was a good neighbor and available without going to church. He had emigrated to America with his villagers and that mattered to the residents of my street.

I liked the feel of my pink rubber ball, the one my friends and I used to play stoopball. This game was inspired by our interest in baseball. The steps on my stoop were the equivalent of a baseball bat. When the guy "at bat" hit a step on the stoop, the ball could be an out if caught by the opposing players on the "field." If well hit it could sail over everyone's head and land by the front door of the Chinese laundry for a home run. Six players, three on each "team," were enough to have a game.

Stickball was another game inspired by baseball. My rubber ball was used to play this game too. The broom of the broomstick was removed and the stick remained. It was our "baseball" bat. The street was our Yankee Stadium or Polo Grounds. Three bases and home plate were chalked out. If a car was parked in our newly created playing field, we would push it out of the way in "foul territory." The Braves would then remove their maroon and gold jackets and each was ready to become another Joe DiMaggio. If a car came by, the outfielder would shout "hold it." On a rare occasion we broke a window and the outfielder would command us to run away with a cry of "cheese it."

One day I inhaled coal dust for the first and last time. My friend Louie Jap told me we could make a quarter each shoveling coal in Mr. Jim's basement. I had found a roll of eighteen dollar singles once and took the money to my grandma, but I had never worked for money. I was delighted to have earned my quarter and brought it home to grandma. I was a man at last. When she told grandpa, he went into a rage, the only time he ever got angry with me.

"I will disown you if you ever do that again."

Grandpa must have known something I didn't know.

On One Hundred and Sixth Street Louie and I would stop by the house where Burt Lancaster, a Hollywood actor, had once lived. We went inside the hallway and noticed that his parents must still live there because their name was on the mailbox. The hallway had a nice clean smell. In late August of every year of my early childhood grandma and I went to the "Five and Ten" on One Hundred and Sixth Street to buy my school supplies. The smell of those pencils and papers still lingers in my nostrils.

STORES, HOUSES
AND THE GANG

The kids in my neighborhood called their apartments "houses" and their tenements "buildings." They called One Hundred and Seventh Street "a Hun Seven Street" and their club, the Braves, a "gang."

My "house" was located on the fourth floor of 319 East, "a Hun Seven." Three other families had "houses" on my floor. The door to my "house" could be opened with a key that was over four inches long and one and a quarter inches wide. The door opened into the kitchen, the largest room in my "house." The kitchen had one big window facing a back alley. Beneath the window was the bathtub; it had a metal cover when not in use. Next to the bathtub was the sink and next to the sink was the water closet. My small bedroom had a window facing the back alley. I sometimes saw Angela, my Italian neighbor across the alley, undressing herself with her shade up. My grandmother's clothesline extended from my back window to Angela's. We had a parlor with a piano and sofas.

The parlor had two windows. One window faced the fire escape and the other window grandma and I used to see what we could from the fourth floor of our building. I saw skyscrapers at a distance. That window gave us a clear view of the Witch's "house" across the street. My grandparents had the small bedroom facing the street. That room had a bed, a chest of drawers, and a big safe. We were fortunate to have heat and hot water. Some of the "houses" were cold-water flats. My friend Louie Jap and his family had to share a communal toilet and bathtub with others living on their floor. Sometimes Louie went to the bathhouse on One Hundred and Tenth Street to take his bath.

My brother Alfred enjoyed going to the city-owned bathhouse, too. It had showers as well as large tubs. Hot water was plentiful and towels were luxurious. Bathers walked on tiled floors. "It was a paradise for us kids," Alfred remarked to me in a recent interview. I never went to the bathhouse. My baths were taken in grandma's kitchen.

In the peak years of the Italian migration to the tenements of East Harlem, apartments sometimes became "boarding houses" where four-room flats were living quarters for many individuals. Before I was born my grandfather's relatives stayed in his small apartment. During hot Summer nights many Italians slept on fire escapes or stayed out late talking with neighbors on tenement stoops.

One and two-family houses were restricted to a few locations in East Harlem. Most were on One Hundred and Sixteenth Street. Middle class Italian Americans occupied these comfortable dwellings. Most were doctors and lawyers. There were public housing projects in East Harlem but for some reason residents of my block looked down on these facilities.

My tenement was infested with pests. Grandma tried to keep her apartment clean but pests found their way there. Mice and roaches were a problem. One of the most terrifying moments of my childhood was the morning I woke up to find bedbugs crawling all over my body. I screamed for grandma. She attacked the bloodsuckers that morning and I never again shared my bed with these insects. There were hushed rumors that rats lived in the darkness of the cellar but I never saw them.

The largest store on One Hundred and Seventh Street was a slaughterhouse near First Avenue. Grandma bought her freshly killed chickens there but never entered the store. She would shout her order to the butcher from the door of the establishment and he would hand her the newspaper-covered chicken at the door and collect his money.

St. Benedict was housed in a small store near our tenement. I asked grandma why he was not taken into St. Ann's Church but was held outside the church while the mass was being said for him on his feast day. "Wasn't he a Catholic?" I asked her. She told me that years ago during his feast day he was taken into the church for mass but the priests refused to allow him to leave. The San Fratellesi had another statue of the saint built for them in Italy and never again allowed this statue to enter the church. After my conversation with grandma, she took me to St. Ann's and sure enough there was the original statue of St. Benedict.

The people of San Fratello worship other saints, including Alfio, Filadelfio, and Cirino, but only one of their saints, Benedict, came to East Harlem with them in the late nineteenth century. Not all saints were immigrants, I thought.

During St. Benedict's feast day he was paraded along the streets of Black Harlem as well as along the thoroughfares of East Harlem. African Americans were amazed at the sight of Italians holding aloft a statue of a Black man. The thirties and forties were decades of intense institutional racism against men and women of color. But Italians came from a country where discrimination was based on regional differences rather than on skin color. And Sicilians especially understood the stigma of discrimination since they had been the slaves of Roman oppressors and more recently the victims of North Italian domination. Italians would only share American racial bigotry when they had been taught American racial preferences. By that time Italian East Harlem no longer existed. African Americans handed the Italians five and ten dollar bills which were then pinned on the saint's vestments. They were generous to a fault.

"Why is St. Benedict black?" I asked my grandmother.

"He is black because he had bugs in his hair," she told me. "His mother couldn't remove them no matter how hard she tried. So in desperation, she immersed him in a cauldron of boiling water and the bugs were killed."

"Why wasn't he killed, grandma?"

"Don't be silly, my son. He was a saint. He couldn't be killed. It was a miracle."

St. Benedict was greater than even Superman and Batman, I concluded.

My grandmother did not know the true story of St. Benedict the Moor. Before the Church canonized St. Benedict, San Fratello was called San Filadelfio. Fratello in Italian means brother and in the early nineteenth century it was renamed in honor of Benedict, a brother in the Franciscan Order. He was the son of Christopher and Diana, African slaves who worked on the estate of Vincenzo Manasseri of San Filadelfio. Benedict was born in 1526. When Benedict was ten years of age, Manasseri emancipated him. Joining the followers of Jerome Lanza, a Franciscan, Benedict became a hermit. Although Benedict never learned how to read and write, he rose to a top position in the Franciscan community of Palermo. A miracle worker, pilgrims came from Italy, Spain, Portugal and elsewhere to worship with him and get his blessings. He died in 1589. In 1883 the Catholic Church of New York City opened on Bleecker Street the St. Benedict the Moor Church for African Americans. It was later moved to West Fifty-third Street. Eventually the congregation became Spanish primarily. The Italians of East Harlem didn't know that such a church existed.[10]

There were other stores on my block: a poolroom for the racketeers, three candy stores, a shoe repair shop, a barber, a Chinese laundry, a pastry store, a grocery store, an Italian cheese store, and two stores where the immigrants met and played cards and talked about the Old World. I never saw the Chinese man and his wife leave his store. Perhaps he went out in the dead of night. Louie Jap took his family's laundry there but my grandma did her own with her scrub board in the bathtub.

The iceman had his place of business in a cellar across the street from our tenement. He was a big man and carried large blocks of ice on his shoulder with a mat separating his shoulder from the ice. Grandma had an icebox and was a regular customer. She would call her order from our window and the iceman would climb four stories to bring her the cake of ice. He was always sweating and cooling himself at the same time. As a child I enjoyed watching the drops from the block of ice in the icebox fall into the basin. Sometimes I counted the drops until I got bleary-eyed.

Grandma did most of her shopping along First Avenue where there were small shops and horse drawn wagons with Italian produce for sale. She carried what she could in her black shopping bag. When she was at the first floor of our building , she would call my name and I would go fetch her groceries. I was a teenager at the time and didn't shop with her anymore.

There was an indoor garage on my street and two lots, one was empty until a playground was built and the other was an outdoor garage with a shack where the Braves often met on cold winter nights. During the winter of 1941–1942 the Braves spent many hours talking about the war and the fifty-six game hitting streak of Joe DiMaggio in the previous spring and summer. Every detail of the streak was remembered. The streak began on May 15 and ended on July 17. He fanned five times during the streak and thirteen times during the entire season.[11] The Braves did pay their respects to Ted Williams who finished the season with a .406 batting average.

I was a New York Giants as well as a Yankees fan. My favorite baseball player was the great catcher Ernie Lombardi. Born in

Oakland, California, the son of Italian immigrants, Lombardi played for the Oakland Oaks before joining the Brooklyn Dodgers in 1931. After one season he was traded to the Cincinnati Reds, where in ten years he amassed one of the greatest records in baseball. In 1938 his batting average of .342 led the National League and he was voted the Most Valuable Player for the year. Cincinnati sold Lombardi to the Boston Braves in 1942 and in 1943 he came to the Giants for a three seasons stay. It was at the Polo Grounds that I saw the great man play. He was the slowest runner in baseball but got on base with his devastating bat action. Lombardi rarely struck out. After his death he was voted into the Baseball Hall of Fame.[12]

Since indoor spaces were not large, the Braves liked to stay out of doors. Even in winter when we couldn't stay in the shack we stayed warm by building fires near the sidewalk.

The boys on my street were inseparable. Three guys from One Hundred and Thirteenth Street joined our gang. There were eighteen regular members of the Braves. Sometimes other kids from East Harlem joined us temporarily. We played stickball and stoopball on our block. We went swimming and played softball at Thomas Jefferson Park. In our late teens we played ball in Randall's Island. We took long walks on the East River Drive and smoked cigarettes on the pier. We necked with the girls at birthday parties held at Maxie's apartment.

Many of the kids on my street went to the Boys' Club on One Hundred and Eleventh Street between First and Second avenues. We played games there and adults told us stories. I joined the Navy

Cadets, a youth club linked to the Boys' Club and housed in the same building. I wore a sailor outfit and participated in marching drills.

Joey Cardillo was a sick kid but he was included in all of our activities. Joey, Johnny Jew Boy, Louie Jap and I enjoyed playing Poker at Johnny's flat. I sometimes played Poker with Louie Jap's family, the Maniacci's, in their apartment. Louie's father, a bookie called Cary Grant, never participated but Louie's mother Rose did along with Louie's sister. I felt a part of the family. I was so close to Louie that members of his family called me his "mother."

Frankie Carbo considered himself our leader. Lefty believed he was destined to replace Stan Musial of the St. Louis Cardinals when the great baseball player retired. Jimmy knew everything there was to know about professional sports and Maxie knew everything there was to know about sex. Mondo was our authority on comic books. After school some of the Braves worked. Lefty, Johnny and Bobby were newsboys. Only three Braves, myself included, graduated from Benjamin Franklin High School. Most of the kids went to vocational schools.

Following World War II a few families from San Fratello migrated to the United States and some of these families settled on One Hundred and Seventh Street. Among the newcomers were two boys my age and they joined our gang. Alfred and I were fluent in the language of the San Fratellesi and we greeted them in our dialect. We were surprised that we were more fluent in the dialect than they were. They couldn't believe that Alfred and I were born in the United States and had never visited San Fratello. In Fascist

Italy, they informed us, it was forbidden to speak dialects even at home. Everyone in Italy had to speak, read and write in Italian. We replied that in New Deal America everyone was encouraged to speak, read and write in English. English had become the common language of the Italian Americans. However, we were never forbidden by teachers, government officials or the police to speak dialects at home out of respect for our grandparents.

"You enjoyed more freedom in America under President Roosevelt than we did under Mussolini," one of the newcomers said.

SICILIAN FOLKLORE
AND AMERICAN COMICS

Saturday nights were special. Louie Jap and I went to a kiosk on the corner of One Hundred and Fifth Street and Second Avenue to buy the Sunday edition of the New York Daily News. We liked to follow the exploits of Dick Tracy as he battled criminals who were so evil that they were usually physically deformed in some unique way. In late December 1943 and continuing into early the following year square-jawed Tracy and his partner Pat Patton were battling Flattop, an assassin with a flat head and droopy eyes. Flattop was a caricature of Peter Lorre, a popular actor at the time. There were moments when the comic-strip detective looked like a goner but he managed to survive against the odds. In the end Chester Gould, the cartoonist, ended Flattop's life in a drowning.

We took our comics seriously and enjoyed following their adventures. (During a newspaper strike in New York City, Mayor Fiorello LaGuardia, knowing how important comic strips were to kids, read the Sunday funnies on radio.)

Before I was introduced to comic strips and comic books, I was introduced to Sicilian popular culture by my grandmother. We would sit for hours in the kitchen while she would spin stories about a fictional Sicilian prankster named Firrazzanu. He was a mischievous scamp who usually got the better of others. Here in Sicilian is a tale she told me on more than one occasion:

Firrazzanu e Chiddu di l'ova

'Na vota Firrazzanu scuntrò unu chi vinnia ova; lu 'mpinci e cci dici: "A vui cull'ova, su frisci?"

"'Nca viditili." Pigghia Firrazzanu, e cci fa mettiri li vrazza tuttidui 'ncucchiati, e cci dici: "Aspittata un pizzuddu quantu mi nni addiju 'na zuzzina." E chi fa? Cumincia a nesciri a unu a unu l'ova di lu panaru e cci li metti supra li vrazza. Chiddu cci cridia. Quannu cci parsi a iddu ca chiddu cull'ova 'un si putia arriminari cchiù, cci sfigghia li causi e si nni va. Ddu puvireddu si vitti sciddicari li causi e si misi a gridari; ma lu fattu è ca cchiùchi gridava cchiù genti s'arricugghianu, e videvanu a stu cristianu ca pi 'na manu si strincia tuttu p' 'un si fari vidiri comu lu fici sò matri; e pi n'autra manu avia lu scantu ca muvennisi cci cadevanu tutti l'ova e facia 'na frocia.[13]

Firrazzanu and the Egg Seller

At one time Firrazzanu met a man who was selling eggs; he stopped him and said: "You with the eggs; are they fresh?"

"Take a look". Then Firrazzanu tells the merchant to fold his arms and says: "Wait a moment while I select a dozen." And what does he do? He begins to remove one egg at a time from the basket and he places each egg on the merchant's folded arms. The merchant was gullible. When it was clear that the merchant could no longer move, he untied his pants and left. The poor merchant saw his pants slide to the ground and he began to shout; the more he shouted the greater the number of people who came to see what was going on. And they saw this man tightening his body to one side so that the onlookers would not see how his mother had made him; and fearing that movement on his other side would allow all the eggs to fall, making a frittata.

One morning after grandma and I had finished our pane e latte (chunks of grandma's bread dipped in milk and a small amount of Italian coffee for flavoring) , she told me another Firrazzanu story:

Lu Vinti Pir Centu

'Na vota un Principi riccuni, mittemu lu Principi Partanna, avennu tanti censi di 'siggiri e nun cci putennu arrivari, pinsau di fari Pricuratori a Firrazzanu. "Te' ccà," dici, "te' la pricura e 'siggi pri mia; ed eu ti dugnu lu vinti pri centu." Firrazzanu si nn'ha jutu a ddu paisi, unni avia a 'siggiri li censi, e fa chiamari a tutti li dibituri. Chi fa? si fa pagari la sò parti, veni a diri lu vinti pri centu, e nenti cchiù. "Lu censu, dici, cci lu pagati a 'n'au tru annu a lu Principi; pri ora vaiativinni." Torna nni lu Principi: "Chi facisti, Firrazzanu? 'Siggisti tutti, li censi?"

"E chi 'siggiri e 'siggiri! a mala pena potti 'siggiri li mei."

"Chi veni a diri?"

"'Siggivi a stentu la parti di lu vinti pri centu chi tuccava a mia; la parti vostra," dici, "ca vi la paganu l'annu chi veni."

Cunsidirati lu Principi comu arristau! Ma si vosi zittiri, e finiu di pigghiarisilla à risata; e Firrazzanu si nni iju allegru e cuntenti.[14]

The Twenty Percent

Once upon a time a rich prince, the Prince Partanna, had so many rents based on the census to collect and unable to do this work himself, decided to make Firrazzanu his collector. "Take this," he said, "take this proxy and collect for me; and I will give you twenty percent." Firrazzanu went to the village, where he had to collect the money, and he called all the debtors. What did he do? He makes them pay the twenty percent and no more. "The rest," he says, "you will pay to the prince next year; for now you can go."

He returns to the prince. "What have you done, Firrazzanu? You collected all the rents?"

"What collection and collection! With difficulty I collected mine!"

"What does this mean?"

"Signore, with difficulty I got the twenty percent belonging to me; your part they will pay next year."

Think how the prince reacted! But he remained silent and then he laughed it off; and Firrazzanu went away happy and contented.

Grandma and I would enjoy a good laugh after each of the Firrazzanu stories.

Illiterate women had passed on orally poems in the dialect of the San Fratellesi from one generation to the next and grandma knew her dialect poetry. Here is a favorite poem of hers:

L'Amata

O Figghia, chi sai bedda, chi sai brauna!
Sa reina fecc taua nun mura mei;
Cam l'auliva nun mura la frauna,
Tu manch tramuri si bidozzi chi hiei
U mar d'agn aura batt dauna;
Chiù chiempi o crosci, chiù bedda ti fei.
O quant è la taua grazia ch'abauna!
Cau chi pussier a tu, ni muoir mei [15]

The Loved One

O daughter, you are beautiful with your golden hair!
That unique face never changes;
Like the olive doesn't change the branch,
Your beauty does not change.
The sea every hour creates waves;
The more you live and grow,
The more beautiful you become.
O how abundant is your grace!
Who possesses you does not die.

Grandpa told me Sicilian fables with important moral lessons. Here is a fable he told me one day as we were riding the subway on our way to Coney Island. He told me the fable in the dialect spoken by the San Fratellesi. I have translated it here into English:

Wind, Water and Honor

One day in ancient times Wind, Water and Honor met as they were walking. They embraced and talked about what they had done and what they would like to do.

Water told the story of the time it transformed itself into a river, irrigating gardens, powering windmills and giving joy to thirsty people.

Wind said that it also powered windmills and without it sailboats could not sail, and later when it had nothing else to do, it went for walks with the clouds amid trees and on mountaintops.

Honor said: "I cannot perform miracles like those you describe, but I hold men in my fist, and though I appear to be nothing, when a man possesses me he possesses a great deal."

After their conversation Wind said: "Where can each of us be found for another meeting?"

Water replied: "Find me in the fountains."

"And if they are dry?" asked Wind.

"Then you can certainly find me in the sea."

Water asked Wind where it could be located.

"When I am free from work, you can find me on top of Mongibello where I play with the clouds."

Wind and Water turned to Honor and asked where it could be found?

Honor replied: "That is not a valid question. If you lose me just once, you will not be able to find me again."

Popular Sicilian fables involved Giufà introduced in Sicily by

the Arabs. Giufà is a simple man who often triumphs over authority figures. One story I remember my grandparents telling me
begins with Giufà looking at the clouds and the moon. Sometimes
the clouds hide the moon and sometimes they do not. Giufà says
"come out" and "stay hidden" to the moon repeatedly. Two thieves
skinning a calf hear these cries and assume someone is warning
them that the police are coming and flee leaving the dead animal
behind. He takes the calf to his mother. The next day she tells him
she sold the meat to flies and they will pay him later. When they
don't come Giufà goes to the judge and tells him the story. The
judge orders him to kill the next fly that he sees. A fly lands on the
judge's nose and Giufà punches it as the judge had ordered him to
do.[16]

Sicilian fables featured Jesus transforming himself into different
animals; princesses restored to life after being beheaded; saints
with human failings. In one story Saint Peter stole pork from a
friend. Indeed, in the real world saints were "hired and fired" by
Sicilians. In 1624 a terrible pestilence ravaged Palermo. Their
patron saint, Cristina, had not protected the inhabitants from the
pestilence and many died. The people of Palermo removed Saint
Cristina from her position of protector and made Saint Rosalia
their new patron saint.[17] In Verga's short story "Guerra di Santi"
published in 1880, villagers fight over who can protect them from
a cholera epidemic, San Rocco or San Pasquale. Saints played
important roles in the lives of poor Sicilians before and after the
unification of Italy.

My grandparents introduced me to history with their accounts of the Sicilian Vespers. In 1282 the Sicilian people rebelled against their French oppressors in what came to be known as the Sicilian Vespers. My grandparents told me that the French couldn't pronounce a Sicilian word and were killed because of that deficiency in their speech. In their accounts of this popular uprising they never told me that Spanish oppressors replaced the French oppressors. As a child I believed the conclusion of this rebellion was an independent Sicily ruled by Sicilian freedom fighters. Years later, my grandfather said, Garibaldi, "the greatest leader in history," convinced the Sicilians to join a united Italy. And they joined willingly because of their high regard for Garibaldi.

East Harlem didn't have puppet theaters but grandpa and grandma had been exposed to puppet theaters in Sicily in their youth and knew many of the stories presented by Sicilian puppeteers. My grandparents introduced me to stories based on the chivalry the Normans transplanted in Sicily. Since my childhood I have been fascinated with Charlemagne and his paladin court. Norman stories often reappear in American comic books. Verga's Don Candeloro, a puppeteer, is one of the most unforgettable characters in Italian literature. My behavior toward women was influenced in part by the puppet theater stories I learned from my grandparents in East Harlem. The idea that women deserve respect was a part of my Sicilian-Norman education in New York.

Many of the Sicilian fables would be considered science fiction stories in our time. I became a storyteller since I was exposed as a child to Sicilian folklore. I invented stories as a child for my friends. I became an historian in my adult years. Historians are storytellers with university degrees.

When "Snow White and the Seven Dwarfs" opened in movie theaters in New York City, my mother came to my street for a visit and took me to see the film. I didn't mind the looks of the Queen but I became frightened and closed my eyes tightly when she transformed herself into the Wicked Witch. I had never realized before seeing this film how wicked witches really were. I was now concerned since we had a witch living across the street from our building.

I asked grandma if there was cause for alarm. She didn't think so since we had large horns right above our door in the kitchen. She told me that if the Witch was near me on the street I should quickly make the sign of the cross. Was she ever married? Did she have adult children living elsewhere? Had she given birth to little wicked witches? What were her super powers? Did she come from San Fratello? Grandma told me nothing about her. She simply told me not to worry about the Witch.

When our witch went out and that was rare, she was covered in a black shawl, long black dress and black shoes. Only her face was visible and she had a perpetual smile. She shopped along First Avenue with a black bag. She lived alone and never had visitors. With my binoculars and from my fourth story window, I had a clear view of the Witch who lived on the third floor of her building. She spent most of her life observing people from her window. And she smiled no matter what. She even smiled when there was thunder and lightning. When that happened I imagined flashes of light coming out of her white hair. One day she vanished. I couldn't believe that the Witch was no longer sitting at her window observing humans and planning wicked things for them. I asked grandma where the Witch had gone? She told me not to worry. We would never see her again. She had been taken by the Devil.

The Protestant Americans came into Italian East Harlem to challenge the folklore and superstitions of the Italians because these beliefs were considered obstacles to Christian teachings. By 1934 there were four Protestant churches in East Harlem. They were located on One Hundred and Sixth, Eleventh, Twelfth and Fourteenth streets. Before these mission churches were established, a Canadian woman, Anna C. Ruddy, founded the Home Garden where boys in the neighborhood were exposed to Bible study. Norman Thomas, a Presbyterian minister who later made an international reputation for himself as a socialist, was the chairman of a federation of Presbyterian churches and social agencies in East Harlem. Writing in 1918, Thomas was pleased with the work of Francesco Pirazzini, pastor of the Church of the Ascension on One Hundred and Sixth Street. There were more than seven hundred members in that congregation. "As Christians," Thomas noted, "our deepest concern is to bring the spirit of Christ to bear upon those conditions of fundamental injustice in our industrial life which keep men from earning a living wage; which deny them any sort of democracy in industry, and then expect them to use political and religious democracy wisely."[18]

Dr. Leonard Covello, my principal at James Otis Junior High School and Benjamin Franklin High School, was influenced by Protestant missionaries in East Harlem. In his letter to me dated February 24, 1975, he wrote: "Miss Anna C. Ruddy, founder of what is now the LaGuardia House at 116th St. and 2nd Avenue, is written up in my autobiography. She picked us off the streets of East Harlem and the church we attended was the Lexington Avenue Baptist Church, a beautiful red brick building in what was a high-class residential area of brownstone one-family houses. The Italian community was east of this area. When we attended church, Sunday school etc. on Sundays we boys used to walk literally on tiptoes and in silence! Miss Ruddy's mission was at 114th St. near First Avenue, now part of Jefferson Park. When I was with Miss Ruddy one of her associates wanted me to go into the ministry. I gave it consideration but there were so many doubts in my mind as to my religious beliefs and convictions that I held off."

When I got older, Superman, Batman, Captain Marvel, Captain America and other superheroes replaced my interest in local witches and the exploits of Firrazzanu. I must admit, however, that Batman's enemy, the Joker, had a wicked smile that reminded me of my witch in my early days with comic books. I bought my comic books in a candy store on First Avenue between One Hundred and Seventh and One Hundred and Eighth streets. The store carried Superman, Batman, Captain Marvel and Captain America titles and these were the heroes I followed. One day I noticed on the wall above the comic book shelves a calendar featuring a drawing of a gorgeous brunette sitting on a suitcase with her thumb out looking to be picked up by a motorist. She had her right shoe in her left hand and her skirt was high enough to see the tops of her nylons. The calendar of the Elvgren beauty left an indelible mark on my view of feminine beauty. I decided that when

I grew up I would want to marry a woman with shapely legs. I did.

One of the first comic books I bought for ten cents printed in 1942 was titled "Remember Pearl Harbor." The cover shows a giant Uncle Sam rolling up the left sleeve of his shirt as he walks over a flaming Pearl Harbor chasing Japanese planes returning to their bases. Inside the comic book there is a picture of a green serpent with the head of Tojo assisting Japanese dive-bombers in their attack on Pearl Harbor. I related to the last story titled "Johnny Remembers Pearl Harbor!" Mr. O'Ryan runs a grocery store and asks Johnny, a blond teenager, if he would like to work after school delivering groceries to his customers. Johnny turns down the offer claiming he has too much homework. Johnny says to himself: "I had to use that homework excuse. I don't want to work after school. Shucks, it's no fun." When he arrives home, he learns that his older brother Tom has volunteered to join the army. Johnny wants to do his part to help his country after Pearl Harbor. He takes the job at O'Ryan's grocery store and with the money he earns he buys a five-dollar defense saving stamp. He is a member of a stamp collectors' club and he convinces his friends that the best stamps to buy are defense stamps. Like Johnny, I bought defense stamps in my school and believed I was making a contribution toward winning the war. The stamps I bought were quarter stamps.

I enjoyed comic books featuring western heroes. Lone Ranger titles were among my favorites. In the May 1948 comic titled "The Lone Ranger" the legendary Masked Man and his faithful Indian companion Tonto defeat a gang of cattle rustlers in the town of Red Mill and put ringleader Carmody and his henchmen behind bars. The Lone Ranger never used his weapons to kill his opponents, only to disarm them.

I liked Disney's "Three Caballeros." I saw it twice with Louie at the Rex. For a radio amateur contest I wrote a comedy skit on this movie only my three caballeros were Jimmy Durante, Lou Costello and Bob Hope. I got two of my junior high school friends to play Costello and Hope while I did an impersonation of Durante. I was told to take the script to the director's apartment on Seventy-second Street. I rang her bell and she appeared in a negligee that left nothing to the imagination. She took the script and thanked me and closed her door. I reached the conclusion that writing about cartoon characters and comedians might not be such a bad idea and for some time after seeing all the director owned I thought I might make a career of it.

I bought myself a joke book titled *The Good Humor Book*, edited by Robert Rango and published by Harvest House in 1944. It claimed to be "A treasury of choice jokes and gags, cartoons and comic drawings, puns and patter, limericks and ditties, anecdotes, riddles and repartee, and many other types of humorous prose and verse." The first joke in the book:

Customer: "To what do you owe your extraordinary success as a house-to-house salesman?" Salesman: "To the first five words I speak when a woman opens the door. I always ask: 'Miss, is your mother in?'"

I convinced my grandparents to buy me a typewriter and asked my classmate, Maxie Rabinowitz, who liked to call himself "The

Mad Russian," to come with me to Bloomingdale's to select a machine. I thought my friend Maxie knew everything that mattered. I told him I was inspired to be a writer by the woman in the negligee. He told me I should see how sexy some women can be in nylons. At Bloomingdale's the Mad Russian selected for me a portable Underwood. It was advertised as a "silent" typewriter. It was not but I put it to good use over many years. However, I never wrote scripts for radio shows.

No one on One Hundred and Seventh Street had as large a collection of comic books as my friend Mondo. His father was a lifer and his mother was hard on him and that may explain why he enjoyed living in a fantasy world of superheroes. His building smelled of garbage and I didn't like to go to his apartment but his comic collection was irresistible. He had comics under his bed, on top of his bed, in his closet and in drawers. Louie Jap and I considered his flat a neighborhood trading post where we exchanged comics regularly.

Comic book superheroes appeared on the silver screen. Our neighborhood movie theater, the Rex, located on Second Avenue between One Hundred and Seventh and One Hundred and Eighth streets, had an admission charge of ten cents for each ticket. On Saturday matinees it played two feature films, five animated films, a prize-giving horse race short and a chapter serial often featuring a comic book superhero. Louie Jap liked to sit in the first row of the Rex and we were naturally overwhelmed by the screen. One of our favorite chapter serials was the "Adventures of Captain Marvel." Boy radio broadcaster Billy Batson was transformed into mighty Captain Marvel by saying the magic word "Shazam." The magic word "Shazam" stands for Solomon, Hercules, Atlas, Zeus, Achilles and Mercury, whose powers are transferred to Billy from a 3,000 year old wizard before he dies. His opponent is the Scorpion, the leader of a gang that wants to capture the five lenses that when placed in an instrument called the Golden Scorpion will give its possessor superhuman powers. Every week a chapter in this cliff hanging serial was played. In the final episode Professor Bentley turns out to be the Scorpion. Bentley had put all five lenses together in the Golden Scorpion and was disintegrated when a ray from the instrument hit him.

Popular comic book and comic strip superheroes appearing in chapter serials at the Rex included Flash Gordon, Dick Tracy, Jungle Girl, Superman, Batman, Spy Smasher, Red Ryder, Zorro and the Green Hornet. One of the greatest pulp magazine villains appeared in "Drums of Fu Manchu," a Republic chapter serial released in 1940.

I traded with Mondo my "All Star Comics" no. 3 for his "Whiz Comics" no. 2, the first appearance of Captain Marvel. Dr. Thaddeus Bodog Sivana, an evil scientist, appeared in this important issue. Captain Marvel eventually had a family of superheroes including Mary Marvel and Captain Marvel Jr. It was thrilling for me as a boy that a simple utterance of a magic word made a superhero out of an ordinary kid. I continued to follow the Captain Marvel stories as an adult and over time one of my favorite Captain Marvel enemies was Mr. Mind, a green worm from another planet. In "Shazam!" no. 9 for January 1974 Mr. Mind captures the Hate Projector but needs to rally the worms of the world to direct their united hatred against Captain Marvel. Captain Marvel naturally defeats the army of worms by creating a rainstorm forcing the worms to scatter rather than keeping them in one location for concentrated hate power. He humiliates Mr. Mind by taking him to jail in an empty can of tomatoes. Of course, I didn't know as a child that I was reading comics that years later were considered Golden Age comics and would become prized collectibles. In 2000 a copy of "Captain America" no. 1 sold for $265,000.

Cartoon characters were popular on radio adventure programs in the early forties. My favorite was Terry and the Pirates. I would first hear the sound of a gong. Then cymbals and coolies jabbering. Then the announcer would say, "Terrreee and the Pirates! Quaker Puffed Wheat Sparkies present Terry and the Pirates." In 1943 Terry Lee and Pat Ryan join forces with the Dragon Lady to destroy a Japanese supply depot under the control of a Nazi. This was almost as exciting as a comic book story I read in which Superman defeats a Nazi named Fange who controlled serpents he had discovered in the Atlantic Ocean!

Like comic book superheroes my friends and I had more than one name each. My name was Salvatore but I was known as Sammy, Sal, Sally and during my obese period Sammy Fat. Louie was Jap. Johnny was Jew Boy. Joe was Corky. At times some of the guys did dangerous things like Maxie Spick climbing the outside of his tenement for three stories. Were we trying to emulate superheroes? Maxie's father was an avid collector of

Superman titles. Did Maxie read these comic books and try to emulate the great superhero? I believed he did!

Of course, like Firrazzanu we enjoyed playing pranks, too!

THE RACKETEERS

One Hundred and Seventh Street in Italian East Harlem was flanked by two rows of tenements opening at First and Second avenues. The tenements gave the block the appearance of a walled medieval town somehow replanted in New York City. The street was the piazza of our East Harlem paese and the poolroom was the place where our racketeers congregated. The poolroom was owned by Wabs. The statue of our patron saint was housed in a store opposite the poolroom. Next to St. Benedict's store was an indoor garage where the racketeers kept their cars, each racketeer had a Cadillac and a Pontiac. Benny Salsice was the exception. He preferred the Chevy.

In the first fifteen years of the twentieth century the most powerful Italian immigrant racketeers in East Harlem were two brothers, Gennaro and Giosue Gallucci. Gennaro, the older brother, lived in the same building as his married brother, at 318 East One Hundred and Ninth Street. They owned a bakery on the ground floor. Gennaro was shot to death in 1909. Giosue continued to increase the family fortune in East Harlem. His many businesses included

bakeries, ice shops and shoe repair stores. He owned many tenements. He was in control of most gambling operations in the area.
He was influential in political affairs. Competitors shot him to
death in 1915, ending the life of a gangster police called the
"Mayor of Little Italy."

To the racketeers of the thirties and forties, however, the Gallucci
brothers were ancient history. Benny Salsice had a candy store.
The back room served as a major command post for the wholesale
merchandising of illegal goods in New York. Miss Bulge owned
another candy store on the block. She was a grumpy old Victorian
lady who had found on my street a refuge from what seemed a life
of misfortune. Both Miss Bulge and Benny had something to hide,
Miss Bulge her past and Benny his illegal enterprises. Louie Jap
and I preferred gregarious Benny to grumpy Miss Bulge. Besides
Miss Bulge had accused me of stealing one of her candies.

"We wanna buy four cigarettes, Benny," Louie said.

"Gonna smoke them on the pier?"

"That's right," I said.

"Try to break the habit, fellas," cautioned Benny as he pulled
four cigarettes from a pack of Camels and handed them to us.
"They will give you cancer when you get to be my age."

But Benny was in his thirties and he looked healthy enough to us
guys.

"Do you want the usual?" Benny added.

"Yeah."

Benny scooped up vanilla and chocolate ice cream balls, pressed
them carefully on sugar cones, and added chocolate sprinkles on

top, all for five cents a cone. The cigarettes were a penny each.

One day he wasn't his usual friendly self. We had come to his store for our ice cream but a police sergeant came in right behind us.

"Scram," Benny told us abruptly.

We didn't know it at the time but learned years later that the sergeant had come that day for his regular pay off.

As a major gangster, Benny had often been in trouble with the law but had served only two terms in jail. More often than not he had bought his freedom from corrupt judges. One judge he knew could be bought for any crime except rape since his daughter had been assaulted once. One crime cost Benny a two thousand dollar pay off. When he was forced to go do time, he bought whatever he needed from his jailers. The guys on the block, myself included, believed that Benny led a charmed life.

Most of the racketeers on my street came from Corleone or were second-generation sons of immigrants from that Sicilian village. Benny Salsice's father was an immigrant from Corleone. Benny and his brother Rosario supported their father who enjoyed staying home with his parrots and canaries. (Al Pacino's grandparents were immigrants from Corleone. They settled in East Harlem where the future celebrated actor was born).

Benny Monk ran small errands for Benny Salsice and other racketeers on my street and they paid him pocket money for these services. Benny Monk had simian features and was slowwitted and hence the nickname "Monk." He was a petty thief as well and the racketeers allowed him to pursue these activities since Benny

Monk didn't know how to do an honest day's work. Benny Monk lived in the apartment next to mine with his two brothers and his mother, a woman in her eighties. She was a pleasant old woman and frequently sat and talked to my grandmother in our apartment.

One day I saw Benny Monk leaving his flat bandaged and bruised with a black eye and I asked Louie Jap if he knew what had happened to him. Louie Jap told me that his father, Cary Grant, had picked up the story of Benny Monk's bad day through the racketeers' grape vine.

Louie Jap told me that Benny Salsice never tolerated men who dared to commit crimes against him. One day he came home to his apartment and discovered it had been looted. He suspected Benny Monk of committing this robbery. Petty theft was what Benny Monk did best. Benny Salsice and two of his henchmen beat Benny Monk to a pulp as he kept denying his involvement in the crime.

"Testa di minchia," Benny Salsice kept hollering at Benny Monk while pounding him without mercy.

Benny always demanded repayment of his loans even from members of his family. Benny's son Pete and his brother-in-law Mike were racketeers. Benny lent Mike a shipment of illegal goods worth $100,000. When Benny's son went to collect the loan, Mike refused to pay. Pete told his father. Benny went to see his father-in-law and told him he would have to pay back the loan since Mike had refused to pay. Benny's father-in-law told Benny he would not pay. That was a fatal mistake. Benny shot and killed his father-in-law but only wounded Mike who fingered Benny to the cops. Benny served a prison term of seven years and was released on the very day his wife died.

In the early 1950's Benny left our street and bought a house in the Bronx. During a vacation in Miami, Florida, he met and fell in love with a rich Jewish widow. They got married and Benny lived in the lap of luxury for the rest of his days.

Rosario was not as successful as his brother. My father's sister Rose had married Rosario. Rosario had worked as a cab driver before going into the rackets like his younger brother. He was a violent man who once hit a rival with a brick. Rosario fathered three sons but rarely saw them. He spent time at Joliet. When my father was dating my mother, an Italian racketeer named Ryan told him to get lost. Ryan wanted no rivals in his efforts to win over Rosalie Cassara. Ryan told Benedict Mondello that he would send his gang after him if he didn't quit seeing Rosalie. Benedict said, "You get your gang and I'll get Rosario's. He's my brother-in-law." Ryan told Benedict that he would stop seeing Rosalie.

Benny Salsice liked to keep a low profile. Tom Mix didn't. Tom Mix owned a tenement on the corner of One Hundred and Seventh Street and Second Avenue. He took two apartments for his own use. He was a lavish spender. He was careless with his money. I found a roll of eighteen one-dollar bills on his stoop and pocketed the money. One day at a bar called the Switzerland on Eighty-sixth Street Tom Mix placed two thousand dollars on the counter and ordered drinks for everyone. An FBI man was there, took a picture and Tom Mix went to jail.

On a roof near my tenement building, Benny Salsice owned a

pigeon coop. He allowed only Gee Gee to fly his prized birds. On summer days when I would go up to my roof, I would watch Gee Gee, stick in hand, flying Benny's pigeons with the same dexterity of a Toscanini conducting the New York Philharmonic. Shirtless, Gee Gee seemed to be doing pirouettes in some intricate ballet with birds.

I never got close to him. I feared Gee Gee. To me he resembled the comic book Human Torch. Muscular and curly-haired, he appeared to have electric currents running through his body. He seemed to be on fire. I learned years later that he was a hitman for organized crime.

My brother Alfred stayed out late one night and was sitting on the stoop when Gee Gee called him from a Pontiac. Alfred noticed that the car had Michigan plates.

"Hey kid," Gee Gee yelled out to my brother. "Come on. I'll take you for a ride."

They rode a few blocks when a police car stopped Gee Gee. The cops remained in their squad car, took one look at Gee Gee, apparently recognized him, and without saying a word the cops drove off.

"They forgot to say good night," Gee Gee said.

Gee Gee had a gorgeous wife who might have been a showgirl in her prime. Dressed in tight dresses, high heels, and a scarf tied around her neck, she could never have been confused with Joan Leslie, an actress who played the role of the good girl in films. She would often stand on the stoop of her building in what seemed to be the posing positions of a Broadway showgirl.

Gee Gee's brother Sammy also made his living as a criminal. Less theatrical than Gee Gee, Sammy was equally lethal if disturbed by someone or something. One evening in the pool room Sammy was involved in a dice game with Bonzo. After Sammy lost two thousand dollars, he ordered an intermission and ran home to fetch more money. His second attempt at victory was equally futile. Sammy was so enraged that he pulled out a knife and stabbed Bonzo in the shoulder. Bonzo was ready to attack him but stopped short perhaps remembering just in time who Sammy had for a brother.

Wabs didn't like altercations taking place in his establishment but he was a violent racketeer. He had hands as big as baseball gloves and he knew how to use them to make a point. Someone working undercover for the FBI had nailed Wabs' friend Jamie in a drug bust. While Jamie was cooling his heels in jail, Freddie the barber was warming his in bed with Jamie's wife. Wabs discovered what was going on. He went to Freddie's barbershop with a baseball bat in hand and broke every mirror and window in the place. Then he sat down and ordered Freddie to shave him. I was standing across the street from the barbershop when I saw Wabs break the store window. My grandmother had taught me never to linger near a crime scene. I walked away from the scene like nothing had happened.

A social worker did something that displeased Wabs. Andy, Wabs' son, got into a fist fight in the playground across the street from my building. The social worker broke up the fight. Andy ran home and reported what the social worker had done. Wabs came to the playground with a bat and crashed it on the head of the social worker. I saw this brutality from my window on the fourth floor of my apartment but mentioned it to no one. Years later I learned from my history books that my behavior was known as the conspiracy of silence practiced by Sicilians. The social worker returned to the playground several months later but he now spoke with a stutter.

Wabs was feared but he was small potatoes compared to Felix the Cat. Few knew Felix the Cat's real name or where he lived. On cold days he wore a camel hair coat and broad brimmed hat. When he entered Benny's store or Wabs' poolroom, everyone stopped talking and stopped moving. Felix the Cat could maintain this silence for five minutes or longer. He would stare out the window and then speak on current political events or the latest world war battle. Everyone listened respectfully, including Benny and Wabs, never daring to interrupt or question him. Once a storeowner on my street angered Felix the Cat. He broke a Coke bottle and slashed the store owner's face.

However, Felix the Cat could be friendly and generous. On Columbus Day 1944 Louie Jap, Johnny Jew Boy, Bobby Mick and I decided to go see Frank Sinatra at the Paramount Theater. The lines were so long that we never got in to hear The Voice. We met Felix the Cat. He took us to Schrafft's and treated us to lunch and some candies.

"Stay in school and read your books," he advised.

Felix the Cat was the best dresser in my neighborhood. One day he gave Carbo, Louie Jap and my brother Alfred a wad of hundred dollar bills to pick up three silk suits he had ordered on Delancy

Street. The guys had never seen so much money in their lives.

Felix the Cat liked to arrange special events at the poolroom. The most memorable billiard match commissioned by Felix brought to East Harlem the Masked Marvel, the legendary billiards player from Brooklyn. The Masked Marvel never removed his mask when performing at a billiards table. He was challenged that Summer night of 1945 by our local champion Marrione. Marrione had played billiards as a child standing on a box in his father's small poolroom several blocks away from Wabs' establishment. Marrione had never been beaten in major events against local talent. Cary Grant collected the bets and turned the purse over to Wabs. Felix the Cat nodded. That meant the game could begin. The game the Masked Marvel and Marrione were about to play was continuous pocket billiards. The winning score established by the contestants was one hundred and fifty points. The Masked Marvel won the lag, so Marrione was stuck with the break. Marrione set the cue ball. Using right-hand English, Marrione tried to clip just a piece of the ball in the rear right-hand corner of the triangle. Unfortunately for Marrione, he left the Masked Marvel an opening. The Brooklyn champion electrified all of us by making one shot after another without missing. Everything was working for the Masked Marvel: his follow through, his draw shot, his left-hand English, his right-hand English. He cleared away the trouble balls first, balls which were clustered together near the rails or away from the rack at the foot of the table. He set up ideal breaks, shots in which the break ball rested only a few inches from the new rack, while the cue ball was only several inches up the table from the break ball. No other contest arranged by Felix the Cat ever equaled this event in the history of the poolroom on my block.

Journalists knew nothing about Felix The Cat but knew almost everything there was to know about Francesco Castiglia. Born in 1891 in Lauropoli, Italy, a town in Calabria, Francesco came to East Harlem with his father at the age of four. His mother came two years later. The family ran a small grocery store on One Hundred and Eighth Street. Francesco did well in school but decided to pursue a career in crime. Like many Italian American racketeers of his generation, he took an Irish name, Frank Costello. Establishing business dealings with Jewish, Italian, and Irish racketeers, Costello amassed a fortune from his legitimate and illegitimate enterprises. During the late 1940's journalists exaggerated his importance as a mobster. He was nicknamed the "Prime Minister of the Underworld." In March 1951 Costello appeared before the Senate Crime Investigating Committee, chaired by Senator Estes Kefauver. As a child he had had a throat operation that left him with a whisper for a voice. Only his hands were filmed during the hearings. His whispered testimony may have inspired Marlon Brando's portrayal of Don Corleone in "The Godfather." He served two jail terms. He died in 1973.[19] On my street the racketeers were indifferent to Frank Costello and his career in crime. Felix the Cat was the gangster they feared and admired.

Some of my friends tried reefers. The racketeers never distributed reefers on the street. It would have been dangerous to sell that stuff on their home turf. Their honest neighbors would have strongly disapproved. But reefers, I imagine, could be bought elsewhere. Some of my friends could have bought them on other streets in East Harlem.

So, in the 1930's and 1940's the racketeers were our neighbors on One Hundred and Seventh Street. Most of the people on my street were not racketeers. When they could afford to leave the neighborhood, they did. The racketeers were the wealthiest men on my street and they left first for better neighborhoods and newer horizons.

THE CLARINET

Dorothy had her magic slippers and the Green Lantern had his magic ring. I had my clarinet. Benny Goodman, Artie Shaw and Woody Herman represented glamour, romance, and enchantment. To me they were larger than life heroes. While my friends wanted to be baseball players like Joe DiMaggio, I wanted to be a clarinetist like Artie Shaw. I couldn't get enough of his interpretations of "Moonglow" and "Star Dust." I was enraptured by the Big Band sound. To be a member of Herman's Thundering Herd was my greatest ambition.

I asked my grandfather if he would buy me a clarinet.

Alfio Cassara came from the land of Verdi and Puccini and believed that music was a part of our soul. He had paid for mandolin lessons for my mother and was willing to pay for clarinet lessons for me. An Italian immigrant who played in a local marching band sold Alfio one of his clarinets. It smelled of tobacco but I liked it anyway.

My grandfather knew a singer named Caruso who sang at the Met. He wasn't Enrico Caruso but he knew professional musicians and recommended Professor Cioè, a violinist with the New York

Philharmonic who had performed with Toscanini.

"Caruso has assured me that Professor Cioè can teach the clarinet," grandpa told me.

The professor maintained a studio in his charming brownstone near Lexington Avenue and One Hundred and Seventh Street. His wife, a tall woman with braids, would let me and my friend Corky, a trumpet student, in and would escort us to the studio, a large room with a piano and late nineteenth-century furnishings. Ten or so minutes later, the professor would enter the room. He was short and fidgety. We would first read music aloud and then play on our instruments. The professor was a stickler for solfeggio. I had to do, re, mi, fa, sol, la, ti before I was allowed to blow my first note on the clarinet. My grandfather hoped I was heading straight for a career as first clarinetist with the New York Philharmonic. I hoped to join the Woody Herman Band and eventually form my own "herd." I admired Herman's flair for catchy numbers. "Your Father's Moustache" inspired me to try to do one better.

Toots Mondello played saxophone and clarinet with the Goodman Band and I wondered if he was related to me. He was not. But I still thought he might put in a good word for a Mondello when I was ready to turn professional. Toots Mondello began to play professionally at the age of fourteen. Not only did he play alto saxophone and clarinet with the "King of Swing," but he recorded with many popular bands, including those of Chick Bullock, Jack Shilkret, Bunny Berigan, Dick McDonough, Miff Mole, Larry Clinton, Claude Thornhill, Teddy Wilson, Louis Armstrong, Ziggy Elman and Lionel Hampton. In the late thirties Toots formed his own band. He led his orchestra in hit tunes including "Thanks for the Memory" and "I'll See You in my Dreams." Toots was a legendary saxophone soloist and was included in the Metronome All Star Band of 1940 recording "King Porter Stomp" with Charlie Spivak, Ziggy Elman, Harry James, Jack Teagarden, Benny Goodman, Charlie Barnet and Gene Krupa. Toots, born Nuncio F. Mondello on August 14, 1911 in Boston, died in New York on November 15, 1992. Pete Mondello, his brother, was not as famous but he played tenor saxophone professionally with Woody Herman's Thundering Herd Band. I hoped I could get Toots or Pete to give me some lessons in playing jazz on the clarinet.

I was thrilled when I learned that our junior high school band would march in the Columbus Day Parade. For weeks we practiced marching tunes. On the day of the parade, I lost one of the keys on my old clarinet as we were marching. It was a struggle for me to continue to play but I faked it where I could. Weeks later, grandpa bought me a better model, an "Anthony Special."

I was determined to make a name for myself in the world of music and I practiced every day I could. But most of the time I was playing lessons' music and not jazz.

I played clarinet in the James Otis Junior High School Band and later in the Benjamin Franklin High School Band. When I was in 8B1, I participated in The Good Neighbor Festival sponsored by the Lions Club of Yorkville. It was held in the Benjamin Franklin High School auditorium on Saturday, May 25, 1946, beginning at 2:30 p.m. Twenty-two schools participated in this event, intended to honor school children in the eight, ninth and tenth grades. Ten of the twenty-two schools represented were parochial schools. I had practiced for weeks on my clarinet. With Santo Cutrone, who was in 9B1, we played "Dance with a Dolly" to a packed house. Directed by Fannie Wolff, the James Otis Junior High School musicians featured our clarinet duet, a saxophone duet, and trumpet and accordion solos. Rudolph Lucchese of 9B2 finished our part of the program with a drum solo. It was my finest hour as a clarinetist.

Top musicians came to Benjamin Franklin High to entertain us. Many came from Harlem. The entertainer I remember best for her artistry was Hazel Dorothy Scott. In December 1940 she had performed Liszt's "Second Hungarian Rhapsody" at Carnegie Hall. During the performance she began to turn it into a jazz number and the audience enjoyed it. She did this again at her performance at Franklin High. I had never heard anything like it. She was a beautiful woman and some of my buddies commented on her looks after her performance. Why she came to a school like Franklin High is a mystery to me. Perhaps she valued the integrated racial conditions encouraged by Dr. Leonard Covello, our principal.

A memorable high point of my musical career came one Friday afternoon when the James Otis Junior High School Band played to a packed auditorium. The audience had come to hear the trumpet playing of the legendary Red DiStefano, a graduate of James Otis and Benjamin Franklin High. Miss Fannie Wolff had drilled us for two weeks for our participation in this program. We began the show with numbers made famous by Artie Shaw, "Begin the Beguine" and "Moonglow." Mr. Alfred Burger, our choral director and a fine tenor, sang "Temptation." Then Red DiStefano appeared on the stage and was greeted with tremendous enthusiasm by the audience. He looked like the twin brother of Red Skelton, the Hollywood comedian, but nearsighted with thick glasses. From the orchestra pit where I was sitting, he appeared almost blind. He put his lips to the mouthpiece of his trumpet and he suddenly became an ethereal being. He began with "Estrellita," then he did "I Cried for You," his third song "I Had the Craziest Dream" brought the audience to their feet. And then he finished his historic perform-ance with "Stardust." I would have never imagined that anyone could play that tune better than Artie Shaw, but Red did. The audi-ence was so moved by his performance that applause and shouts of "encore" resulted in Red's rendition of "Frenesi" and "Deep Purple." There were shouts of "Harry James" as he left the stage, a thin redhead with thick glasses and a trumpet in his left hand.

At Franklin and at Otis we had Spring festivals. One of the best took place on May 26, 1949. In Part One of the show, the kids from Otis in the glee club and band ensemble performed seven Italian songs plus "America, I Love You." Part Two belonged to us, the singers, dancers and band players at Franklin. We did "Flying Down to Rio," "Softly, as in a Morning Sunrise," "Latin American Fantasy," "Jalousie," and "La Carioca." Part Three fea-tured an "Evening at Radio City" with "Stardust," "In the Still of the Night," "Dancing in the Dark" (a dance solo by Gerard Kennedy), "With a Song in my Heart" (sung by Salvatore Greco), and "It's a Grand Night for Singing" (band and choristers). The Finale, "Let All the Nations Rejoice," from "Cavalleria Rusticana." We had outstanding stage sets put together by four students.

Artie Shaw's rendition of "Indian Love Call" was one of my favorite numbers. It begins with the drum beating followed by Artie's clarinet. I asked Rudy Lucchese, the great Franklin drummer, if he would play the number with me. He agreed. We arrived ten minutes before band practice one day and we went through the number. Fannie Wolff heard us play and told us to do it for one of our assembly periods. We did and I felt like Artie Shaw that day with the great Gene Krupa backing me up. A magical moment.

I wasn't discouraged after hearing DiStefano because he played trumpet and I played clarinet. But in James Otis Junior High, I met two guys who played clarinet brilliantly. Ronnie Naroff played both tenor saxophone and clarinet and Santo Cutrone played clarinet. Their playing was simply flawless. I realized I could never play like them and music became a hobby for me to be enjoyed. My grandparents were not unhappy when I told them of my decision. They told me lawyers and doctors made more money. I continued to play tarantellas for my grandmother and that pleased her very much. Her favorite, "The Wedding Tarantella." However, I did stop taking private clarinet lessons.

THE SCHOOLS

Italian East Harlem was a dying community in New York City. It was also the largest Italian American community in the country. It existed after Irish and Jewish East Harlem and before Spanish East Harlem. As a child I was taught by my grandparents to speak dying languages in my dying neighborhood. Out of necessity I would become a cultural transient.

The Sicilian language and Sicilian culture were not considered important enough to be maintained in the United States and Italy in the 1930's and 1940's, my childhood years in East Harlem. Fascist Italy and New Deal America could find no place in their societies for the culture of the Sicilians. Ironically, Sicilian culture enjoyed a period of rebirth in the early twentieth century led by a playwright with an international following, Luigi Pirandello. His plays in the Sicilian language were performed in the Teatro Nazionale in Rome, the Teatro Olympia in Palermo, the Teatro Mastrojeni in Messina and elsewhere in Italy before the Fascist period. Often the leading male roles were played by Angelo Musco, an important Italian actor of that era. There were other important Sicilian authors writing in the Sicilian language, including Alessio DiGiovanni, who wrote *Lu Saracinu* and other books.[20] In my schools I was taught to write in English and in Italian. I was discouraged to speak or write in what was called "dialect Italian." Sicilian, a language only second in importance to Italian in Italy, was considered a dialect in the United States and Italy, a language to be abandoned rather than nurtured. The Sicilian language was the language of poets in Emperor Frederick II's court in Palermo before his death in 1250. And Dante and Petrarch recognized Sicilian as the first Italian literary language before the Tuscan contribution. The Italians lost a bilingual opportunity and a literary jewel when they gave up the Sicilian tongue.

What was the Sicilian culture lost to Americans and Italians when their political and educational leaders abandoned the language that expressed it? Leonardo Sciascia's writings on this subject give us valuable insights. It is a temperate culture. It is a culture that values the natural environment. It is a culture in which the past, present and future have little meaning for they meld into one. It is a culture that knows man's limitations. It is a culture that distrusts authority figures. Many Sicilians had hoped following the unification of Italy that a common language, Italian, learned by all Italians, would make all Italians politically equal. Sicilians have always believed that a better world must exist outside Sicily, an idea that encouraged emigration to other lands. Sicily is a melting pot of many ethnic groups that eventually became Sicilian. It has been Greek, Roman, Norman, Arab, Spanish, and more. Since the Risorgimento, it has become Italian. Over the centuries the Sicilians have shown their pessimism, however, in the Sicilian language itself, a language that has no future tense. Since Sicilians have been conquered by many invaders who have controlled their political institutions and have acted for them, the Sicilian male believes he can only rely on himself; he is a man alone. Sicily, the largest island in the Mediterranean, a sea that exists at the center of so much history, "cannot be anything else but a land of conquest and devastation."[21] Lawrence Durrell in his visit to the tiny island of Ortygia off Syracuse found the remains of a Greek temple cocooned within a Catholic Church; Sicilians do not destroy symbols of their past but rather accommodate these icons. Durrell found vestiges of the Greek way of life in the "food, the wine and the wild flowers of the land they had inhabited and treasured." Andrea Camilleri, a contemporary Italian writer of "gialli," Italian murder mysteries, writes in Sicilian-Italian and is one of the most popular writers in Italy today. Perhaps we are seeing an interest in the Sicilian language and culture among the general reading public in Italy. Perhaps a Sicilian writer was correct when he wrote many years ago:

Senza Italia, Sicilia si nni scanta;
Senza Sicilia, Italia picca cunta.
Without Italy, Sicily would fear foreign invaders.
Without Sicily, Italy would count for little.[22]

I grew up in a family that spoke both the Sicilian language and a Sicilian dialect. I knew very little English. When I was enrolled in P.S.168, the elementary school on One Hundred and Fifth

Street, I was placed in a class set aside for children who were considered difficult to teach. My classrooms had desks and chairs riveted to the floors. The building was old and gray with a high fence in front of the entrance. Some of my teachers were patient with children like myself and some were not. When I didn't understand Miss Rundge's instructions on an astronomy assignment and brought in the wrong work, she held my paper up to the class and humiliated me in front of my fellow students. I remember one day we were placed in two rows, one for the girls and one for the boys. We were going to assembly. I held the hand of a cute girl named Frances who happened to live on my street. The hand holding on that fateful day convinced me that she was the Snow White of my dreams. I was too shy to tell her that. I remained her secret admirer for many years after the hand holding incident. I was Dante and she was my Beatrice. In my autographs graduating album she wrote: "To Sally, Best Wishes and Lots of Luck. Friend Frances."

I was friendly and interested in learning and I adjusted very well to my elementary school. I was the only boy to hold a graduating class office, the treasurer's position. In my yearbook I listed history books as my favorite readings. I wanted, however, to be an entertainer when I grew up. Miss Arnowich was my favorite teacher. She wrote in my yearbook: "To a typical American boy, my very good wishes for the happiness you so richly deserve. It has been a genuine pleasure to have known you this past year. May we continue our friendship."

At James Otis Junior High School (P.S.172) and at Benjamin

Franklin High School, I came under the influence of Dr. Leonard Covello, the principal of both schools. Covello was born in Avigliano, Italy in 1887. In 1890 Covello's father emigrated to East Harlem, where his wife and children joined him in 1896. Leonard Covello was influenced by Protestant social activists, Anna C. Ruddy and Norman Thomas, whose Presbyterian church on One Hundred and Sixth Street he attended. He studied at DeWitt Clinton High School and Columbia University. In 1944 he completed his doctoral dissertation at NYU. In 1911 he took a position as a teacher of French and Spanish at DeWitt Clinton High. He participated in numerous Italian cultural organizations. Covello campaigned for years to establish a high school in East Harlem. It became a reality in 1934 after winning the political support of Congressman Vito Marcantonio and Mayor Fiorello LaGuardia. James Otis Junior High and Franklin High were all boys schools. Led by Leonard Covello and Mario Cosenza, the Italian Teachers Association of New York City in 1922 campaigned successfully to have the Board of Education place Italian on a parity with the other foreign languages taught in the high schools. In 1938, 567 students in Benjamin Franklin High School alone were taking Italian. Francesca DiMaria taught me Italian at Otis; Dina DiPino taught me Italian at Benjamin Franklin. Dr. Covello believed that Benjamin Franklin High as a community-centered school "cannot only present to the immigrant the best in American culture and traditions, but also imbue him with the worth of his own culture." Learning Italian culture and the Italian language were vital to the success of students and their parents. This learning would "mitigate the Italo-American sense of inferiority by gaining for the Italian student and Italian group, social and ethnic status and probably a decrease in discrimination through the concept of the cultural worth and prestige of Italian civilization." Franklin High had other minority students as well and their needs had to be met too. Franklin was considered by its founders as a "fluid, experimental school and must have its entire personnel saturated with the spirit of experimentation and willingness to be anything and do anything for boys." Teacher education programs at New York University and Columbia University were initiated under the direction of Covello to meet the needs of the high school. Covello became a teacher, he wrote me years later, because "books were a passion with me." In 1972 Covello joined the Sicilian social reformer Danilo Dolci to work as a consultant with Dolci's Center for Study and Action in Western Sicily. Covello died in Sicily in 1982.[23] I was influenced by that "passion" for books. Daniel Patrick Moynihan, a Franklin graduate, may have been influenced by the liberal political philosophy that guided Covello, Marcantonio and LaGuardia.

Fiorello LaGuardia was elected to the Congress in 1916 representing lower Manhattan, but he became a national figure in the 1920's when he represented East Harlem in the Congress. He supported a liberal program of social reform, including equal rights for women, old-age pensions, unemployment insurance, workmen's compensation, public housing and an end to child labor. The Norris-LaGuardia Act prevented the use of antilabor injunctions. He took office as mayor of New York City in January 1934 taking his liberal programs to City Hall.[24] In that year Benjamin Franklin High School, a major LaGuardia goal, was opened to boys in East Harlem.

Vito Marcantonio, closely associated with Covello and LaGuardia, had been a major supporter of a high school in East Harlem. Born in East Harlem in 1902, Marcantonio was a radical political reformer, to the left of both Covello and LaGuardia. In the early 1920's Marcantonio became LaGuardia's campaign manager. Like LaGuardia, Marcantonio spoke Yiddish, Italian, and Spanish. Elected to Congress in 1934, Marcantonio was to the left of Roosevelt's New Deal supporting the rights of miners and agricultural workers. He supported civil rights for African Americans as early as 1941, when he lobbied unsuccessfully for a federal antilynching bill. Marcantonio was the only congressman to oppose American intervention in Korea. Marcantonio supported Communist Party positions but was not a Communist himself. Since he supported bread and butter programs, the voters in East Harlem kept sending him back to Congress. Marcantonio died of a heart attack in 1954.[25]

Associated politically with Marcantonio and LaGuardia was Edward Corsi, a liberal reformer and advocate of immigrant causes. Corsi was born in 1896 in the Abruzzo village of Capistrano, Italy. His father, a politician, died early in Edward's childhood. Edward's mother remarried and the family migrated to East Harlem. Edward graduated from St. Francis Xavier College and Fordham University Law School. Committed to competent government and social justice for immigrant groups, he organized a Theodore Roosevelt Club in East Harlem. In the 1920's Corsi was appointed director of Harlem House, located on One Hundred and Sixteenth Street. Harlem House, later renamed LaGuardia House, offered social and educational programs designed to prepare immigrants for citizenship in the United States. President Hoover appointed him United States Commissioner of Immigration. Under his friend LaGuardia Corsi became director of New York City's Emergency Home Relief Bureau. In 1943 Governor Thomas E. Dewey named Corsi Industrial Commissioner for New York State. In that post he called for the liberalization of unemployment insurance. In 1954 Secretary of State John Foster Dulles named him special assistant on refugee and immigration issues. He ran unsuccessfully twice for political office. He died in a car accident in 1965.[26]

On June 24, 1947 I graduated from James Otis Junior High School, School District No. 10 in East Harlem. Four other Braves graduated: Joseph Orefice, Frank Rescigno, Louis Russo, and Mondo Santangelo. Another graduate, Antonio Salerno, lived on One Hundred and Seventh Street but never joined our gang. I won the Italian medal for best student in that subject and Louis Russo won the medal for best student in monitorial service. An Irish kid, Patrick Donohue, won the medal for excellence in English. James Velez was the best student in mathematics and another Puerto Rican, Mario Fernandez, was the top student in social studies. My best friends in school graduated with me: Michael Andreani, Anthony Platania, Max Rabinowitz and Charles Palazzo, the top student at James Otis. Palazzo won the medals for scholarship and science. There were no African Americans in my junior high school. In a graduating class of one hundred and sixty two, the Italians numbered one hundred and nineteen. Dr. Covello delivered the "Message to the Graduates":

As you leave us to go to one of the senior high schools or vocational high schools of our city, you will carry with you the best wishes of the principal of your school. As you go on to your higher training, we want you to succeed in several ways:

1. Make a good all around record in school. That means doing your lessons well and maintaining good attendance.

2. Preparing as soon as your time comes, to honestly and diligently take your place in the world of work; not looking for a soft snap.

3. Conducting yourself like a good sport—that means not being small and mean.

4. Becoming the kind of person people will be glad to have around.

5. Learning to think and to act in a friendly way towards people who are different from you.

6. Keeping in mind that your mother and father will depend more and more upon you as you grow older. Don't let them down!

These are a few of the things that we would like to see you achieve.

At Benjamin Franklin High School Dr. Covello took an interest in me and I participated in programs with him. He did radio programs in the Italian language and I was selected with two other students to participate in a few of his programs. Miss DiPino would prepare us for each participation. Dr. Covello took me to a class he was conducting in teacher education at New York University. I spoke to his students in English and Italian. I found a sophisticated environment at the university, an environment I had never thought existed. Years later, Professor Francesco Cordasco told me Dr. Covello considered me a son.

One day in my Italian class Miss DiPino was drilling us in Italian vocabulary.

"Salvatore. How do you say 'a little' in Italian?"

"Tanticchia," I said in Sicilian, without thinking.

"Salvatore!"

"Un poco."

"Much better."

Teachers at Benjamin Franklin, including Charles Calitri, were introducing me to American and English literature. I was allowed as a top student at Franklin to take Calitri's course titled "American History and Social Problems in the Light of American Literature." The aim of the course "is to acquaint students with the thoughts and attitudes of outstanding American authors on current problems of American democracy." The course was intended to offer not only "literature but intercultural knowledge." I remember how shocked we were when Charlie announced that he was an Italian Jew.

"You gotta be kidding," Louie Russo replied. "There are no Jews in Italy."

Calitri had a sport jacket that was torn at the elbows. He didn't have enough money to buy a new one. But he kept writing novels until he became a successful author.

In my senior year I ran for the position of secretary on the Ben Franklin Party with Louis Russo who ran for the position of president and John Marsalisi, who ran for the position of treasurer. We put out a sheet of paper which stated, "Vote vote vote vote down the row of the stars." We won the election hands down.

I remember Blacks in large numbers in the band. Blacks dominated our basketball team. I remember a Puerto Rican, a kid named Mercado, who played clarinet and oboe like he was born with these instruments in his mouth. Many Puerto Ricans were on drugs. Often the Italians did not mix well with either African Americans or Puerto Ricans. I did make friends, however, with Black guys, including a big fella named Henry Booker, who played basketball for Franklin.

I remember telling a Black saxophone player in our band that I thought Joe DiMaggio was the greatest baseball player ever. He disagreed and told me he believed Ted Williams was the best. I wondered why Black kids didn't have Black baseball players they could admire. They did but I was not aware of it at the time. I thought quite incorrectly that they didn't have great jazz clarinetists like Benny Goodman, Artie Shaw and Woody Herman. Because I played clarinet in the high school band, I made many Black friends. Black guys were numerous in the orchestra. They were also very ambitious. Julius White, President of the Frederick Douglass Society, wanted to be a psychiatrist, Ernest Osborne,

Captain of the Science Squad, hoped to become a dentist, Floyd Hawkins wanted to be an art teacher, Charles Elliott intended to pursue a career as a musician, and Henry Booker, Captain of the Varsity Team, wished to become a pharmacist. The aspirations of my Black high school friends were greater than the aspirations of my friends on One Hundred and Seventh Street. Black Harlem was more stable than Italian East Harlem and kept its professional leaders. East Harlem did not. Black professional fathers and mothers encouraged their children to become professionals and remain in the Black community.

Across the street from my high school at One Hundred and Sixteenth Street and Pleasant Avenue was a small grocery store that sold hot meatball sandwiches on Italian bread. Once a week during lunch period three or four of us would go there to eat those incredible meatball sandwiches. The tomato sauce was heavenly.

Frank Sinatra came to our school to talk to us about racial and religious intolerance. The auditorium was packed that day with students and teachers. At the end of his talk he sang some songs for us. A year or so later he made the movie short, "A House I Live In." His message was now on film. It was the first time that I had heard an entertainer talk about the need to fight discrimination. I thought it was wonderful to be an entertainer like Frank. I didn't know then that Frank was a Sicilian American.

My Franklin yearbook for 1950 had an optimistic tone to it. We were hopeful for the future. Dr. Covello wrote that "it is in our power to eliminate poverty, to crush hatreds of other people, and to establish the real brotherhood of man." One of the graduates, Nick

Syragakis, wrote a futuristic letter dated May 23, 1999 and noted: "Most of the old evils are dead and buried. Instead of armies we have brotherhood, cooperation and progress."

I graduated from Franklin High in June 1950 with the second highest average in my class. I gave the salutation address at commencement. I spoke about the support parents and teachers had given the graduates over the years. I told them, "This graduation today is your show. You people out in the audience have directed and produced it. I sincerely hope you will enjoy it." (My grandfather, grandmother and mother attended.) A Greek kid, Nicholas Syragakis, got the highest average and delivered the valedictory address. I had learned to write and read in Italian as well as English in the schools. I was proud of my Italian American identity even though I had never seen Italy. I was no longer a Sicilian American. I began to feel embarrassed by my grandparents who had a culture considered inferior by the teachers I respected. And I was no longer a Brave anchored on a "Hun Seven" street. I was starting my freshman year at New York University in the fall. Franklin had prepared me for a cosmopolitan world outside East Harlem. I had met and befriended kids of different cultures and I had acquired a respect for Italian culture and traditions. As an Italian I could influence and enjoy the world outside East Harlem. As a Sicilian I could not.

THE MOVIES

The Rex was dark and damp. It had a stage because it had been used by Italian vaudevillian performers in the first years of the twentieth century when it had been managed by the notorious female racketeer Pasquarella Spinelli. I liked to go to the Rex on weekdays when I didn't have school. The Rex was convenient for me since it was around the corner from my street. I would check the lobby cards to see what was playing. I would buy a ticket if low budget westerns of the early 1930's were being shown. My generation called these movies cowboy films. They were in black and white, my favorite colors for films.

I would try to get to the theater early in the afternoon, often as soon as it opened. Few patrons came to see these films in the early afternoons and I enjoyed sitting in a nearly empty theater in the dark for ten or fifteen minutes before the film was played. This was a moment of privacy for me. East Harlem was congested and noisy. The Rex gave me a respite from these conditions.

There were many cowboy stars I liked but Tim McCoy was my favorite. He was short like me but his large white hat, not quite as large as a sombrero, made him appear taller. His shirt and pants were black. He rode a proud stallion named "Pal." He was clean-shaven and polite and always removed his hat when greeting a lady. But what I enjoyed most about his films was the absence of a musical soundtrack. There were moments of silence in his movies. Sound was introduced at the appropriate moments: when people talked, when horses' hooves hit the dirt in the road, when punches were landed in fist fights, when guns were fired, when a whiskey bottle hit a whiskey glass.

Tim McCoy returned to his wife Helen after years of amnesia in "Texas Cyclone," a film in which John Wayne played a supporting role. Utah Becker had hit Tim McCoy in the head causing the loss of memory. Becker was not clean-shaven and never fought fairly. Tim fought the final and decisive gun battle with Becker after Becker announced that Helen was leading an immoral life.

Jack Holt was another one of my favorite early cowboy stars. I was pleased that Dick Tracy looked like him. To me it made Dick Tracy a square shooter like Jack Holt. I enjoyed reading western novels as a teenager. Among my favorites were Fran Striker's The Lone Ranger and the Outlaw Stronghold and H. C. Thomas, Red Ryder and the Adventure at Chimney Rock. Red Ryder is described as "tall and tanned and leather-hard."

My favorite writer of westerns was Ernest Haycox. His short story "Stage to Lordsburg," was adapted for the movie "Stage-coach" starring John Wayne.

When I was a kid, I went to the Saturday matinees at the Rex with the Braves. We had to sit in the boys' section and the girls sat in their area. We were very noisy and the matron, a big woman in a white uniform, kept aiming her flashlight at us while hollering "Keep quiet." One Saturday we were there to see "Keep 'em

Flying" with Abbott and Costello. The unexpected surprise in that movie was Martha Raye. She played identical twin waitresses and drove Lou Costello bananas when one sister gave him the free pie and the other sister told him to pay ten cents for it. But what impressed the guys the most was her figure especially when she sang and danced to "Pig-foot Pete the Boogie-Woogie Man." Louie Jap nudged me during the song and said, "Her face is for the birds but she's some tomato. Look at that ass."

Most of my impressions of the Second World War came from the movies I saw at the Rex. With my friend Louie, I saw John Wayne in "Flying Tigers," "The Fighting Seabees," and "Back to Bataan." The battles appeared exciting and American soldiers appeared heroic. I was proud of an uncle of mine who served in the army and survived a head injury. He lived with a metal plate in his head for the rest of his life. Unfortunately, he became a battered husband.

Some of the films I saw must have had the financial backing of a wealthy Italian American banker, Attilio Henry Giannini, the brother of the legendary giant of American banking A. P. Giannini, founder of the Bank of Italy and by 1928 owner of the Bank of America. After practicing medicine, Dr. Attilio Henry Giannini entered the banking profession with his brother. According to Louis B. Mayer, the head of MGM, Attilio Giannini was the first major banker to lend money to motion picture studios. By 1921 most of the major film distributing companies had accounts with the Bank of Italy. Attilio backed financially the production of Charlie Chaplin's "The Kid." He made the first one million dollar loan to Hollywood for Samuel Goldwyn's production of "The Kid from Spain" in 1932. Seven years later, he financed the production of "Gone with the Wind." He served as a mediator in settling business disputes among studio executives.[27]

Many of the films I saw at the Rex and elsewhere had musical scores by an Italian American born in Brooklyn, Salvatore Guaragna. His parents were immigrants from Calabria, Italy. By the time he was registered for school his parents had changed the family name to Warren and his first name to Harry. A self taught musician, he began to find success as a songwriter in the 1920's. He wrote for Broadway musicals but decided to go to Hollywood since movie musicals had become popular with theater audiences. Beginning with the hit musical film "42nd Street" choreographed by Busby Berkeley with music by Harry Warren, he wrote many of the most popular songs of the early twentieth century for films. Among my favorites growing up in East Harlem were "Shuffle Off to Buffalo," "Chattanooga Choo Choo," "I Had the Craziest Dream," and "On the Atchison, Topeka and Santa Fe." He worked for Warner Brothers, Twentieth Century-Fox, MGM and Paramount. The popular hit "That's Amore" was written for Dean Martin. He was financially successful but received little recognition for his musical accomplishments. He avoided publicity. He wrote primarily for movie musicals and his works were buried in the credits.[28]

Some of the films I saw in New York theaters were directed by a fellow Sicilian, Frank Capra. Capra was born in Bisacquino, Sicily in 1897. The family moved to a poor Sicilian neighborhood in Los Angeles. Frank was the only one of his parents' fourteen children to attend college, graduating as a chemical engineer. He found jobs as a gag writer first for the Hal Roach studios and later for Mack

Sennett. Capra's first box office hit, winning five Oscars, was "It Happened One Night" released in 1934. It established a new type of film, called the screwball comedy. His major movies were fables like in the Sicilian tradition. In "Mr. Deeds Goes to Town," released in 1936, an honest but naïve man wins his battles against corrupt authority figures.[29]

Louie and I liked Humphrey Bogart in gangster roles. Bogart looked great with a cigarette dangling from his lips. On the One Hundred and Seventh Street Pier, Louie spotted two chicks. He asked me for a cigarette without taking his slanted eyes off the skirts. He took two puffs from the Lucky Strike and said: "Wait here." With the cigarette dangling from his lips, he approached the girls and talked to them for what seemed an eternity to me. When the girls walked away, he flicked the butt into the East River and came back to where I was standing. "We got dates with those chicks for Saturday night at Jefferson Park". That Saturday he had a great necking session with his date. My girl was a divorced woman with a child and she devoted all of our time explaining why I was too young and inexperienced for her. I struck out. Grandma would have been relieved had she known how my date had turned out.

My mother would occasionally come to One Hundred and Seventh Street to visit my grandmother and those were the only times I saw her. My grandmother always had high praise for my mother and I grew up considering my mother a woman of impeccable values. However, grandma had nothing good to say about my father. To me dad was Dracula married to Snow White. She would take me to the movies in places that looked even better than the castles I saw in my picture books. She took me and my brother Alfred to see "The Adventures of Robin Hood" at Radio City Music Hall. I thought that Olivia deHavilland's Lady Marian had the same high standards of moral behavior as my mother. The live stage show, "Stars at Midnight," featured the Music Hall Corps de Ballet and the Music Hall Rockettes. Perhaps it was at that moment that I reached the conclusion that a beautiful woman had to possess shapely legs.

When I stopped going out on Sundays with my grandfather, I started going to the movies on Sundays with my friend Danny, his mother and his older sister Mary. They treated me like a member of their family and I grew to associate movies with family outings. I had a Sunday family. They always went to the Loew's Seventy-Second Street Theater. The ceiling looked like a starlit night. After the movies we went to a soda fountain store near the theater. Danny's father never came with us. He was a cruel man who once beat Danny with a chain.

I once tried to interest my grandfather in the movies. He took me to a show at the Star Theater on One Hundred and Eighth Street but he was uncomfortable during the movie and I never asked him to come to the movies with me again.

PART II

A GALLERY
OF PORTRAITS

ALFRED

We were sitting in the kitchen playing a card game named "War." Alfio Cassara sat at one end of the table. My brother Alfred sat at the opposite end and I sat in the middle. Alfred was six at the time. I was seven and a half. I was grandfather's favorite. During the game he kept sneaking aces to me. He assumed my kid brother wasn't aware of what he was doing.

"I quit," Alfred shouted. "You're a cheat," he said to grandpa. "You've been feeding aces to Sammy the whole game."

It was a difficult time for my family. Only my grandfather was working during the Great Depression. My father was bedridden with rheumatic fever. Alfred had asthma. My mother was trying to save her marriage and was in a state of depression as she took care of my father. Grandma ran the household. We were confined to a four-room apartment.

Neglected at home, Alfred climbed on a chair to unlock the latch and ran down four flights of stairs to the street. He did this often during his childhood and became a streetwise kid, more streetwise than I could ever be since I was pampered by my grandparents.

Alfred was short but tough and learned early in life to defend himself. Soon the kids on the block came to view my brother as the kid to beat to gain recognition from their peers.

Mondo was older and taller than Alfred. Mondo had a reputation to maintain since his father was a lifer, a gangster with a killer instinct. Mondo was an avid comic book reader and perhaps wanted to emulate the toughness of the superheroes.

"I'm gonna beat you black and blue," he announced to Alfred one day with some of the guys looking on.

"I wouldn't try that," Alfred responded.

It took ten fist fights for my brother to beat Mondo's vendetta out of him. The guys were impressed and continued to look for opponents for my brother to fight.

A big Italian immigrant kid and his family moved into our block and the guys convinced him to challenge Alfred in a fist fight. Maybe they thought he was some future Primo Carnera. Alfred accepted the challenge and beat his opponent until he yelled "stop." The guys were disappointed with this outcome since they had put so much confidence in the immigrant kid.

Alfred's reputation as a street fighter was soon known by guys living in neighboring streets. He discovered that he had to live up to this reputation or he would be shunned by the guys in the neighborhood. Dominick was a big guy who lived on One Hundred and Sixth Street. He was a smart kid and did well in school. He was older than Alfred and every time he saw him he would either taunt or hit him. Alfred got tired of running away from this bully. He took a kitchen knife from the apartment and when he saw

Dominick coming towards him, he brandished the weapon.

"What the hell," screamed Dominick. "Stop. I won't hit you again."

Our parents and grandparents did not know that Alfred was leading such a difficult life. Indeed, few parents on our street were aware of the lives their children were leading in the neighborhood. The street and the home were two different environments.

My grandfather gave us allowances every week. My allowance was always more than Alfred's and my brother realized that grandpa "was not on my side." But there were men on the street who treated him better. Some were racketeers. Tony Bologna was a local racketeer who gave Alfred money to buy ice cream. One day the cops found Tony Bologna stabbed to death in his bed, a gangland execution.

The old Italian immigrants in my street liked Alfred, too. They played bocce in the empty lot across the street from our tenement building. When it rained, they would dash for cover in a store opposite the lot leaving the balls behind. Alfred would fetch the balls and bring them to the players. As a reward they would buy him a bottle of beer. They enjoyed seeing the little kid drink a man's drink. It gave them a laugh.

Alfred was very good in sports. Stoopball was a favorite game on One Hundred and Seventh Street. All we needed was a rubber ball and a stoop. It was based on baseball. One day Alfred's team played Bobby Mick's team and Johnny Jew Boy, a member of Alfred's side, hit a home run. Bobby got so angry with Johnny that he hit him on the head with the ball. Alfred came to the defense of

Johnny since he was on his team. Bobby was much bigger than Alfred but my brother held his own until two older guys from my neighborhood broke up the fight. Alfred believed you have to support and defend the guys in your corner. It was a matter of honor.

Alfred went to P.S.168 until he was about eight when our parents moved to Brooklyn. Once I was called to the principal's office because my brother was not as attentive in class as he should be and I was asked to talk to him about it. Alfred moved with our parents but I stayed with my grandparents. Alfred started third grade at P.S.123 on Irving Avenue in Brooklyn and graduated after completing the eighth grade. He attended East New York Vocational High School and had an unfortunate experience in his shop class. After the teacher stepped out of the shop classroom, a big Black kid hit Alfred for no apparent reason. Alfred fought back and got the better of the Black student. The other members of the class watched the fight. When the teacher returned, he hit Alfred believing he had started the fight. Alfred had been labeled a bad boy even when he was not. For the remainder of the academic year, Alfred attended all of his other classes but never completed his shop requirement and never graduated. A month later that same Black boy was in the boys' toilet when another Black kid demanded a cigarette from Alfred.

"You ain't getting a cigarette from me," Alfred replied. The Black kid he had trounced in the shop classroom told the other Black kid, "Don't mess with that little man." And that was the end of that.

My brother found a congenial environment in Brooklyn because

Brooklyn had a baseball tradition unmatched by any other place in America. Many amateur teams played baseball in Brooklyn in the pre-Civil War era, when Brooklyn was known as the "city of baseball clubs." Following the Civil War baseball in Brooklyn was played primarily in the Parade Grounds in Flatbush. There were twenty-one baseball diamonds on the Parade Grounds with locker rooms and showers. Amateur teams scheduled their games there and had loyal fans who came to cheer them on. There were ethnic teams named the Celtics, the Polish Falcons and the Italian Lafayette Triangles, teams that competed on the baseball diamonds at the Parade Grounds. The schools had baseball teams. Brooklyn boys grew up "in an environment pervaded by the game." Baseball taught Brooklyn boys the importance of "fair play." Ebbets Field, the home of the Brooklyn Dodgers, a professional baseball team, was small in size and gave the fans an intimate baseball experience. A great rivalry developed over the years between the Brooklyn Dodgers, known earlier as the Robbins, and the New York Giants. The Brooklyn baseball tradition eventually became "the national pastime" leading Zane Grey, the writer of westerns, to conclude, "Every boy likes baseball, and if he doesn't he's not a boy."[30]

When my kid brother was eleven years old, he gave a demonstration of his pitching skills at a booth in Coney Island. Benedict had given his brother Fred money to go enjoy himself at Coney Island and to take Alfred with him for company. A barker in front of a booth was calling for amusement park goers to try their skills at striking down pins with three hard balls about the size of oranges.

Winners were awarded prizes of stuffed animals.

Uncle Fred asked Alfred to try his luck at knocking down the pins. Alfred had pinpoint control when he was throwing a ball of any size. He kept knocking down pins with the first of three balls allowed. The barker kept filling Fred's arms with prizes. Crowds formed and cheered the little kid as he put on a show of throwing control rarely seen even at professional baseball games. "We will hear from that kid someday," shouted a spectator who announced himself as a Yankee fan. Alfred retained this skill at throwing a ball with accuracy as an adult. At a carnival in Easton, Pennsylvania with our father looking on Alfred put on a show by a booth featuring balloons to be popped with balls. Alfred kept winning prizes while Benedict kept getting angrier and angrier since he was unable to pop any balloons and returned home emptyhanded.

Alfred returned frequently to East Harlem to stay with me and our grandparents. He liked Brooklyn more than East Harlem; it was a better neighborhood. Our gang, the Braves, enjoyed his company because of his toughness, fairness in dealing with others and his excellence in sports. The gang's major interest centered in sporting activities and Alfred fit into the group better than I did. He could swim, ride a bike, roller skate, play stickball and stoopball and with a baseball he could throw a fast fastball and a hard to hit curve. He developed bone chips in his pitching arm and was rejected by the armed forces during the Korean War.

Another gang, the Red Wings, was often in trouble with the law and didn't mind pushing around other boys' gangs in East Harlem. They were located in and around One Hundred and Sixteenth

Street. One time they attacked a young cop in Jefferson Park and stripped off his clothes on a lark. Alfred and two other Braves went to the movie theater on One Hundred and Sixteenth. Some Red Wings were sitting in back of them and started to taunt them. The Braves were challenged to a fight when they complained about the taunting. The Braves had to accept the challenge but they knew they were in trouble. The Red Wings were at least one hundred strong while the Braves numbered only eighteen. The Red Wings could fight dirty using zip guns against their opponents. When the Braves appeared with some of the older and bigger guys from our block at the designated battleground in Jefferson Park, the Red Wings backed down, refusing to fight the Braves and their older defenders Foo, JoJo, and Louie Bruno. JoJo grabbed the biggest Red Wing in the mob and challenged him to a fist fight. JoJo won and that ended the confrontation with the Red Wings once and for all.

I dated Betty, the sister of a Red Wing. We necked twice on a bench in Jefferson Park. She liked me and so did her brother, who was my classmate at Benjamin Franklin High.

Lucy was a popular girl on One Hundred and Seventh Street and when she moved to the Bronx, three members of the Braves went there to visit her. Johnny Jew Boy, Gaspar, and Bobby Mick were taunted by the Eagles, the gang of that neighborhood. When they came back to our street, they reported what had happened. My brother was visiting us at the time. The guys decided to go as a group to the Bronx and confront the Eagles. We were eighteen strong when we entered their territory and we were ready to become the kind of juvenile gang missionaries like Anna C. Ruddy had been trying to eliminate in East Harlem since the end of the nineteenth century. I didn't like being there but I had to go or the guys would have considered me "chicken." The Eagles were not willing to fight us and both gangs agreed to establish friendly relations in the future. Alfred played a leading role in establishing good relations with the Eagles. The members of the Eagles liked the challenging way he pitched a stickball game and we had many contests with them in East Harlem and in the Bronx. We came close that night, however, to becoming a violent gang like the Red Wings.

We enjoyed good relations with other gangs in East Harlem because Alfred was viewed as the pitcher to beat in stickball games. The Leopards liked us and liked to play ball against us. Alfred pitched a no hitter in a stickball game against the Leopards. Moreover, he was prominent in Brooklyn as a softball pitcher for a team called the Skulls holding most of their contests in Bushwick Park.

Alfred had his share of dates as a teenager in East Harlem but he was no Casanova like Maxie Spick or Louie Jap. Anna liked Alfred. He dated Anna and I dated Connie and the four of us went to neck at the RKO Eighty-Sixth Street movie house. (Connie's father owned the outdoor auto parking lot on my street.) When Alfred refused to continue seeing Anna, she complained to me and asked for my assistance in this matter. Nothing came of it.

In his late teens, he would visit East Harlem in his used 1950 Nash and pack his car with as many as nine passengers for rides in the neighborhood.

Alfred worked for our father in the grocery store on Knickerbocker Avenue and discovered what a poor businessman our father was. Benedict extended credit to customers who could never afford to pay him. (In fact, the more credit he gave them, the more difficult it was for them to meet their obligations.) Alfred began working for our father when he was twelve years old. Our father occasionally beat him for no apparent reason. One day he kicked and punched my brother because he came home a few minutes later than he was ordered to.

Our mother was intimidated by Benedict and never came to Alfred's defense. Benedict had once told Rosalie that when they were in the company of his relatives she was to remain silent. (Rosalie liked to spend many hours in front of her mirror combing her hair and applying make-up to her face.) When Alfred got bigger he raised his fists one day when Benedict tried to punch him and that ended the beatings. Benedict became a better father to his third and fourth sons, Charles and Benedict. They have fond memories of him.

When Alfred got older, he worked for our uncles at the creamery in Stockertown, Pennsylvania and at the Arthur Avenue store in the Bronx and discovered that they were stealing from each other. Chic admitted to his brother Benedict that he was a thief and couldn't help himself. Fortunately, Alfred left these family businesses and made a living as a milk industry truck driver. He had steady work and provided for his wife Mary and his three children, Benedict, Mitchell and Rosalie. Corrupt officials had controlled Alfred's union, Local 584 of the Teamsters. One retired official owned a "bunch of bars" from the money he had pocketed. Fortunately, a new president, Willie Whelan, cleaned up the union and gave the workers an honest administration. Before becoming a labor leader, Whelan had worked as one of the notorious "sandhogs," Irishmen who built tunnels during working hours and brawled and got drunk in the evenings. Whelan, the father of five kids, found Jesus and changed his life for the better. He became a union reformer and spent many hours reading the Bible to prison inmates.

Whelan found a determined supporter in my brother Alfred. When Whelan and his team decided to oust the corrupt union leaders of Local 584, Alfred, employed at the time at Queens Farms, collected money from the workers to support the insurgents. He convinced the milkmen that it was important that the insurgents knew their funds were coming from the workers themselves. Alfred was such a successful fund raiser that the reformers were prepared to offer him a position on their team, an offer he refused. Corrupt leaders of Local 584 asked Lennie, the night supervisor at Queens Farms, to find something in Alfred's background that would lead to his dismissal from the company. Lennie informed Alfred of this campaign to have him fired and told him to be careful. The reformers failed in their first attempt to defeat the incumbents. Four years later, the reformers ousted the corrupt union men and Alfred played a major role in collecting money to finance their campaign. Alfred's fellow workers trusted him, knowing that his motive for supporting the reformers was "justice for the working guy."

When Whelan's reformers called a strike in the Spring of 1979 to improve workers' benefits, Alfred was an active participant. He helped to man the phones and joined the picket lines. The Catholic community came to the support of the strikers. Priests allowed rallies to be held on church grounds. Whelan secured the services of a Catholic priest considered one of the best mediators in such disputes and the strike ended with the workers winning valuable concessions from the bosses.

Alfred also worked for the Waddington Milk Company in Brooklyn. His route supervisor was Willie the Greek. Willie was short and fat. He liked to brag about the racketeers he called his friends. For five consecutive days he greeted my brother by hitting him forcefully in the ribs. On the fifth day Alfred told Willie, "Hit me again, so that I can punch you in the mouth." Willie the Greek never again hit Alfred in his morning greetings.

Alfred met Mary Toto at a White Castle Hamburger Restaurant in Lynbrook, New York and it was love at first sight. They were married on January 31, 1954. I was the best man at their wedding. Mary was born on October 29, 1934 and is the only child of Peter and May Toto. Mary is a high school graduate.

Peter, an Italian American, died when Mary was only eight years old. Peter was an auto mechanic. Since May worked, Mary took care of her father during his long illness. May did house cleaning and worked with a physician to keep herself and her daughter above water financially. May helped Dr. Frank deliver babies. May's father was Charlie Jablonski, a Pole, and her mother, Barbara Murovetski, was Russian. They met on the ship taking them to America and were married soon thereafter. Charlie worked as a roofer. They lived on Mulberry Street in the early years of their marriage. Later, they moved to New Hyde Park, New York. They had five daughters and three sons. One son was killed by a street car and one daughter died in a fire. Alfred and Mary have three granddaughters: Lauren, Dianne and Marissa. Lauren is studying for a doctorate in American literature. Lauren has been brought up in the Jewish faith, since her mother Sandra is Jewish and her father Benedict is not a practicing Catholic.

Mary Toto's family took politics seriously. Barbara Jablonski was a staunch communist and frequently argued politics with her children who supported American democratic institutions. When Barbara's husband was unemployed in the 1920's, she went into the business of making and selling booze to members of her community. Barbara made herbal medicines and these were provided free of charge to sick people in her neighborhood. Barbara was known as one of the most beautiful women in New Hyde Park and one of the most controversial.

May's second husband, Nick Boccalino, was a career soldier and devoted to Mary and May. They lived in a house in Lynbrook that had once been a one-room schoolhouse in another location. Next door was a house that had once been a church. Before the street was paved with tar it consisted of clam shells. It was a safe community and residents didn't lock their doors. When May and Nick moved to Florida, Mary and Alfred bought the house and raised their children there.

Mary and Alfred believe that family comes first. Mary always felt safe when Alfred was with her, knowing that he was always ready to defend her against any danger. He was so devoted to his children that he would "have killed for them" if they had been harmed. Today Mary and Alfred live with their married daughter in Webster, New York and Mary takes care of the household, doing the cooking and cleaning and watching over her granddaughters Dianne and Marissa since their parents work.

Fortunately, I discovered early in my childhood that my father was a man I couldn't trust. One day he berated me on and off for several hours because I had misspelled the word "heart." That scolding changed my life for the better. I decided to live with my grandparents. My brother was not as fortunate.

One day in a hospital Alfred met Clara, the former wife of Charlie, a cousin who had formed a partnership with Benedict in the Knickerbocker Avenue store. Clara was recovering from an operation. She told Alfred, "Your father was weird." I knew that when I was six. My brother realized it much later.

Alfred lived by the Golden Rule but discovered that many of his relatives, including his father, did not. He overcame many obstacles imposed by the family and had to break away from their businesses to save his immediate family and himself from economic disaster. As a child he knew how to defend himself but this was a liability as well as an asset. Champions must always defend their titles, even in ghetto areas.

Alfred lived with his wife and children near my parents' home in Hempstead. My grandparents lived with my parents at the end of their lives. When grandpa got sick with rashes, Alfred took him to the doctor. He treated our grandparents with respect. Grandma told Alfred, "You turned out very good." Street kids usually do.

MARIA

The Circolo Italiano of New York University was holding a birthday party for Frances, a Puerto Rican member of the club. The party was held in Frances's house in northern New Jersey. I had nothing special to do that Saturday evening following a day of serving customers in my father's small grocery store on Knickerbocker Avenue in Brooklyn. I took twenty dollars out of the cash register and told my father I was going to a party.

"I'll catch the last train out of Manhattan for Hempstead."

"Have a good time."

Friday morning Maria was still unsure whether or not to spend the night at her girlfriend's house in New Jersey and then attend the party for Frances the following evening.

"You're not going to meet anyone if you stay home and watch television," Aunt Rose advised.

Maria packed a few things and left for Marie Anne's house. She wore a navy blue dress and matching shoes that broke Saturday morning. Fortunately, she had taken another pair of high heels and that Saturday night Marie Anne drove her to Frances's house.

I arrived later. I knew some of the members of the Italian Club and was greeted by Maria's friend Eda who had invited me to the party. I was new to the club and Eda introduced me to the young men and women I didn't know. I had seen Maria somewhere before but I couldn't place her. I liked her looks. She was several inches above five feet tall, had dark brown hair and eyes and an incredibly gorgeous figure. She had Betty Grable legs. I made sure I got to sit next to her.

We talked and talked and talked. We were interrupted when we all played musical chairs, sang happy birthday to Frances, gave out the presents, and ate the cake. Otherwise, Maria and I seemed oblivious to our surroundings. We talked like old friends or intimate lovers. Two young Sicilians who seemed to know what each was thinking as well as saying. We couldn't hide anything from each other even if we had tried. I could no longer mask myself as an Italian American in her presence. Our Sicilian culture seemed to be creating an umbilical cord connecting me to Maria. It was a moment in time beyond my imagination.

Except for Frances's parents everyone at the party was a student at New York University. Maria couldn't understand why I studied so much. "I cram for my exams the night before," she said. She was a student in the School of Commerce and had a management major and a retailing minor. I was a liberal arts student and I assured her I couldn't possibly cram and pass my courses.

As an undergraduate student at NYU I majored in history and minored in French. I found French an easy language to learn. I discovered to my delight that I had been speaking Sicilian-French since my childhood days in East Harlem. The Normans had invaded Sicily centuries ago and had left their language in towns like San Fratello. Grandma Rosalia had been my first French teacher!

Maria remembered seeing me previously at an Italian Club dance and at an Italian Club excursion to an orphanage. At the party she pretended never having met me before. "That's the kind of guy I'm going to marry," she had told Eda, when she had seen me with a redhead at the dance held a month before the birthday party.

When I said goodnight to her I called her "Marie." She suddenly turned cold and corrected me. We had agreed to see each other the following Saturday. I told her I would take her to Tavern on the Green.

Riding the Long Island Railroad all the way home that night, I could hear over and over again in my mind the song "Maria" sung by Stefano Lombardi on a record grandma had me play on the Victrola on many occasions. It is a song of a lover who wishes to return to his girlfriend Maria. An immigrant song.

I didn't see Maria early next week on campus but I met Carmello and Richard at Washington Square Park on Tuesday. They had not attended the birthday party and I was eager to tell them that I had met a wonderful girl named Maria.

"She's not so wonderful," Carmello cautioned. "She went to our dance class this Monday and danced cheek to cheek with the dance instructor who refused to dance with anyone else. She accepted a date from him. He's going to pick her up at her house in Brooklyn and take her to his dance class at Brooklyn College every Wednesday."

I couldn't believe my ears. My dream girl might be just another chick, like Marcia, the girl I was currently dating.

Later in the week I met Maria in the section of the NYU cafeteria called "the Italian Area" by the students. She agreed to go to the movies with me before our Saturday date. We kissed for the first time in the Paramount Theater in Brooklyn. I remember liking the taste of her lips. This relationship could get serious I thought.

On Saturday evening I picked her up at her house at Bedford Avenue and said "hello" to her father, Joseph Rampello. She was a knockout in her yellow print dress. We took a cab to Tavern on the Green in Central Park and danced, drank and talked the evening away. We necked in the cab all the way back to Brooklyn. I told her to stop taking dance lessons and she agreed without hesitation. We knew we were in love.

Two weeks after I met Maria at Frances's party I proposed marriage to her during a subway ride on the IRT. It was a crowded train. I was standing and she was sitting. I knew she would say "yes" and she did.

She was graduating from NYU that spring while I had one more year of college to complete. We decided to get married in one year, July 31, 1955 to be exact.

Joseph and Lena Rampello were not pleased with our plans. They went along hoping we would break up.

The day after I proposed to Maria, I received a call from Mrs. LaMarca, the owner of the tenement in East Harlem where my grandparents continued to live. Mrs. LaMarca was the only one in her building to have a phone.

"Come quick. Your grandmother has had an accident. She's at

home but is badly bruised."

I arrived at One Hundred and Seventh Street late at night. I hoped I wouldn't see any of my old friends. I felt I had nothing in common with them. I found a deserted street. Few ventured out at night anymore. It had become a ghetto street. I ran up the four flights and remembered my grandfather's cough. I knocked on the big door.

"It's Sammy, grandma."

Grandpa opened the door and I kissed his cheek. He told me grandma was in the bedroom.

She was badly bruised. A kid on a bike had run into her. She kissed me and started to cry. We had a long talk like old times. She told me that when I left them to go live with my parents, I had forgotten to take the cowbell I had asked grandpa to buy me when I was four or five. I told her I had met a nice Sicilian girl and had proposed marriage to her.

"You really should become a lawyer first before you get married," she said.

She reminded me of the day when I was five and got so angry with my aunt who lived one flight above us that I peed outside her door.

I told my grandfather that East Harlem was no longer safe and he should stop working and come live with us in Hempstead. He told me working was in his blood. I left their apartment two hours after I had arrived. The street was still deserted except for two guys speaking Spanish on a stoop where I used to play stoopball with the guys.

As a child I considered my family grandpa and grandma. We had Cassara relatives on One Hundred and Seventh Street but grandma was not on speaking terms with them. She told me never to speak to them, to pretend they didn't exist.

Maria, however, came from a large extended family on her mother's side. Lena Rampello was born Pasqualena Crapanzano, the first child of Peter Crapanzano, a barber, and Antonina Parisi. Lena was born in Raffadali, Sicily, on December 21, 1908. She died in Brooklyn, New York, on September 22, 1981. Lena's parents were immigrants from Raffadali. Antonina's brother, Louis Parisi of Raffadali, was the oldest of six children of a widow. He migrated in the early twentieth century to Brooklyn with the intention of bringing over his entire family later on. He opened a barbershop, got into local politics, became the legal secretary of an Irish judge, and sent for his family. Louis became a ward politician in the tradition of George Washington Plunkitt of Tammany Hall and knew how to deliver the Italian vote for the Democratic Party in his neighborhood in Brooklyn.[31] Louis befriended a Jew in the garment industry. Two of Louis's brothers, Nick and Joe, formed a partnership with Al Sizanski and opened a factory in Brooklyn which made women's coats. They hired immigrant relatives and friends from Raffadali and Jews. The Parisis and Crapanzanos were a part of what historians call a chain migration, meaning people from the same European village migrate to the same location in America and often work in the same business. Louis's two sisters, Antonina and Rose, married two brothers, Peter and Ralph Crapanzano, barbers from Raffadali. Peter and Antonina had six children: Lena,

Vivian, Vincent, Joseph, Ralph, and Rosie, the youngest.

Joseph Rampello, one of Louis's nephews, was an ambitious young man who wished to pursue a career as a coat designer. Joseph was born in Raffadali on October 6, 1905, and died in Brooklyn on November 25, 1974. Migrating to Brooklyn in 1923, Joseph went to work for his uncles in the factory, rising from a machine operator to a designer of women's coats and finally to a partnership in the family business. He married Lena Crapanzano on July 20, 1930 at the Church of St. Lucy Virgin and Martyr located at 802 Kent Avenue in Brooklyn. Maria, their daughter, was born on September 15, 1932. She was baptized at St. Lucy's on April 16, 1933. It was a difficult birth. They had named her Sara after Joseph's mother but his mother considered the birth miraculous and Sara's name was changed to Maria in honor of the Blessed Virgin. (Maria passed away on October 26, 2004 of a sudden heart attack in her sleep.)

Family members worked together in the factory and lived in the same community, moving as a group from the Italian neighborhood on Nostrand Avenue to more affluent, ethnically diverse neighborhoods on Lee Avenue and on Prospect Place in Brooklyn. In the early years they worshipped at the Church of the Madonna of Pompei at 225 Seigel Street.

Louis Parisi's brother Salvatore became a lawyer. A testimonial dinner in Salvatore Parisi's honor attended by several hundred people was held at the St. George Hotel in Brooklyn on June 7, 1931. The affair was sponsored by the Raffadali Society of Brooklyn and the Louis Parisi Association, Inc.

By the early 1950's Joseph and Lena Rampello pooled their savings with those of Peter and Antonina Crapanzano, Rose and Ralph Crapanzano and Vivian and Victor Faro and bought a splendid Victorian house on fashionable Bedford Avenue. "It was like a palace," Lena remarked on June 22, 1979 when I interviewed her. Her family was most important to Lena and family gatherings on Bedford Avenue were her most enjoyable events. Lena, her mother and her aunt shopped for two days before the Christmas Eve family get-together. We were served sausages, cutlets, pasta and meatballs and cakes during the afternoon meal and fish was served at midnight.

Lena came to America when she was ten years old. "Everything was strange," she remembered. She finished only the third grade of schooling and was kept home to take care of her younger brothers and sisters when her mother got sick. The family had very little money and meat was served only once or twice a week. The Italian community on Nostrand Avenue in Brooklyn was friendly and Lena didn't remember any discrimination directed against her. Small shops sold an abundance of goods and food. The Italians celebrated the feast honoring Our Lady of Mount Carmel in July. Her parents were practicing Catholics and were regular churchgoers. They encountered no discrimination when they moved to mixed neighborhoods with large Jewish and Irish populations. "We made it better and better" was her way of describing the economic progress of her family. Family members pooled their resources and bought two cottages on Sound Beach in Long Island and family gatherings were held there during the Summer months.

There were strict rules for courtship. She and Joseph Rampello did not date. They met at her house. She sat at one end of the parlor and he sat at the other end. When it was ten o'clock her father would come into the room winding the clock. That meant it was time for Joseph to leave. Joseph and Lena were allowed to attend weddings and family parties together. She believed that she had plenty of freedom in her marriage. She sent Maria to college so that her daughter could have advantages she was denied. Lena always voted for Democrats. "They help the poor," she remarked and that was reason enough to support them.

Her greatest fright was the day that she learned that her father and her uncle challenged two thieves in their barbershop. The men asked for haircuts and shaves. After they were served they demanded money from the two brothers, both in their seventies. Peter was challenged while he was holding a razor in his hand. "I will cut your faces if you don't get out of here," he told both men. They ran out of the shop without taking any money. It made the newspapers but the brothers were told by family members that they had been foolish to put themselves in such danger over money. Peter and Ralph didn't see it that way.

I asked Lena to explain the reason for her family's economic success. "We acted as a unit," she told me. "Family is everything. When you go outside the family, you have nothing."

For many years Maria was the only grandchild of Peter and Antonina Crapanzano and she was the center of attention. She received gifts from family members. She developed a fondness for all her aunts and uncles but loved Joseph and Rosie most of all.

Maria's relationship with Rosie was impossible to categorize. Sometimes they acted like close sisters. Sometimes they talked like close friends. There were times when Rosie behaved like Maria's mother. One thing is apparent; they trusted each other. Maria admired Ralph who became a dentist and had a successful practice next to the Plaza Hotel in Manhattan. Her father spoke Italian but insisted that his daughter speak English. English was spoken in her family. Her parents tended to be too strict with her and made great efforts to direct her life. Her father called her disrespectful after she offered to teach her mother how to read and write. She attended public schools but eventually was enrolled in Catherine McAuley High School which had a large Irish student body. It was an all girls Catholic school. She had few contacts with boys as a teenager but did kiss a kid named Scott at a birthday party at her cousin Vivian's house. She had such an attractive figure, however, that a boy fell off his bike while looking at her.

I didn't enjoy my college years but Maria did. Since NYU was near Fourteenth Street, a shopping area, Maria spent many hours shopping and pricing items. As president of her house plan, a women's club at NYU, she arranged parties with men's clubs.

With her college friends Eda, Marie Anne, and a Jewish girl named Judy, she patronized an eatery near Washington Square that featured hot apple pie with a cup of coffee. She didn't join the Italian sorority because they were opposed to her Jewish friend becoming a member. Maria's courses were not challenging at the business college and that was just fine with her. She was the center of attention in the school because she was attractive and because there were very few women taking business courses. A young professor made her sit in the front row in class so that he could admire her legs.

Maria turned down many young men who wanted to date her during her college years. She was not interested in casual dating since she wished to date a man she could love instead. She was not casual in her relationships with women. She made strong friendships with Eda Pellegrini and Judy Bernstein in college and Margaret Byrne and Eileen Seidelbach in high school. In Maria's yearbook Eileen wrote, "I'll always miss you being near by." She had strong family ties to her aunts and uncles. Aunt Rosie was like an older sister to Maria. Uncle Joseph was like an older brother. She called them Rosie and Joey. She was like a lioness looking after her son and granddaughter. Maria called her daughter-in-law Joan "my daughter." She was never casual in her dress and appearance. She enjoyed wearing tailored clothing and pearl earrings. Maria enjoyed reading her newspaper and playing Scrabble with me. She told me these were important activities to keep her mind alert. And she was truthful and devoted to me and was always ready to support me in my career. Perhaps these are Sicilian virtues. Grandma Rosalia had many of the virtues I later found in Maria. In Sicilian Maria would have been described as sistematica, a woman who was at peace with her moral decisions and with the people she loved. She liked to call me Sal or Turiddu, a familiar version of Salvatore in Sicilian. Maria spoke the Raffadali dialect.

We courted for one year. When my family first met her family at

Maria's house, called the "Big House," my grandmother made it clear to her grandmother that Maria was getting the better deal. A friendly exchange took place with Antonina standing firmly in support of Maria.

Commuting was difficult as I moved about from Manhattan to Brooklyn and to my house in Hempstead. When Maria asked her parents if I could sleep over at their house in Brooklyn, they said no. Maria threatened to leave the house and they relented.

Maria and I shared the view that sexual relations came only after marriage. Did we think that way because we were Sicilian Americans? In Italian East Harlem boys placed women in two groups. Sexual relations were permissible with girls who were eager to engage in such activities. Virgins were the marriageable women. My grandmother frowned on premarital sexual relations.

A Vilanga, a play written in Sicilian by Nino Martoglio and Luigi Pirandello and first performed on August 27, 1917 at the Teatro Olympia in Palermo, sheds light on old Sicilian views regarding sexual relations. The play features two Sicilian couples. Ninfa, married to Oraziu, pursues passionately Saru, married to Anna, a devoted wife. Ninfa lures Saru into an extramarital affair. After Oraziu discovers this, he forces Anna into having a night of sexual relations with him, threatening that he will kill her husband if she refuses. Saru learns what has happened. Oraziu argues that his night with Anna is a repayment in kind. Saru doesn't see it that way, noting that Ninfa was promiscuous but Anna was not. Saru kills Oraziu.

Maria didn't want a big wedding reception after church services but her mother insisted. That year Maria worked at Blue Cross and was forced to turn over her entire salary to her mother who used it to pay for the wedding reception. Maria was given an allowance every week. The woman who designed her wedding gown gave her a hooped rather than a straight dress. She had measured Maria at a perfect 36-26-36. We were married at Our Lady of Refuge Church in Brooklyn and the reception attended by more than one hundred guests was held at the fashionable Towers Hotel at 25 Clark Street in Brooklyn. Maria wanted the song "Because" played when we entered the hall but got "here comes the bride" instead. Our wedding cake cost fifty dollars. It had a peaches and rum filling and was made by the famous Ferrara Bakery at 195 Grand Street in Manhattan. We couldn't wait to leave the reception.

We didn't have a honeymoon. I had graduated from NYU in May 1955, two months before the wedding. However, I was taking courses at St. Johns University Law School and couldn't take time away from my studies. I didn't like law school and stayed only a summer at St. Johns. I tried the School of Education at NYU for one semester and finally enrolled for the Ph.D. program in history at NYU. For one year I went to school part-time while holding a full-time job with an insurance company on Wall Street. Maria left Blue Cross and became a housewife that year. But she decided to take a job with American Four, an insurance company on Wall Street, because we decided that I should be a full-time student. While most of the graduate history students were young Jewish men, I was impressed that my history professors admired the administrative work of one of their recent graduates, an Italian

American named L. Jay Oliva, who years later became president of the university.

I respected my NYU professors. Ray W. Irwin, Ralph B. Flanders and Bayrd Still taught me American History. Leo Gershoy and A. William Salomone taught me European History. I minored in Eastern European Studies taught by the Polish poet-scholar Ludwik Krzyzanowski. A political exile, Professor Kryranowski was one of my admirers. Since I was an Italian and an enthusiastic student of Polish history, he considered me a friend of Polish freedom and independence in the tradition of Philip Mazzei and Joseph Mazzini. I published my first scholarly article in a journal he edited. I respected most of all A.William Salomone, an Italian American scholar and a brilliant lecturer. Salomone had studied under the celebrated Italian historian and champion of the Mezzogiorno, Gaetano Salvemini. I took Professor Salomone's course in Italian History and I took great satisfaction in knowing that the Jewish men in my class were studying the story of my ancient people.

My friend and classmate Gilbert Osofsky was not favorably impressed with the teaching and scholarship of the NYU historians. He was a brilliant student whom I had known as early as my undergraduate days at the university. He completed his doctoral studies at Columbia University. His dissertation, *Harlem: The Making of a Ghetto*, was published by Harper in 1966. I met Osofsky at a convention where he told me he was working on a study of the Mennonites. He held his last job at Cornell University in Ithaca, New York, where he committed suicide.

During my graduate years at NYU, Maria and I rented a small apartment at 2657 Bedford Avenue, the same street where Maria's parents lived. We had little time for each other. My courses were offered in the late afternoons or evenings and she had a daytime job. A Jewish neighbor, seeing me carrying books all of the time, asked my mother-in-law if I was studying to be a rabbi.

Maria made fifty dollars a week. My grandfather gave me fifteen dollars a week. We ate two times a week at the "Big House." Maria helped me with my research. I received the doctorate in history in 1960. My dissertation examined how American magazine writers reacted to the Italian immigrants from 1880 to 1920. The reaction had been generally negative. My dissertation adviser was Professor Bayrd Still, a scholar who devoted his entire career to working with students at NYU. With our new 1960 Ford Falcon, we left for Trenton, New Jersey, where I was hired at Rider College as assistant professor of history. We were in debt for the first time, since the Falcon cost us $2034.07. It was a lemon from the very start.

We rented an efficiency apartment in a new luxury building on West State Street. It was adequate until Charles was born at 8:02 p.m. on August 23, 1961. It had been a difficult pregnancy for Maria and we decided that Charles would be our only child. When he was a toddler he was always looking to play with me, so I had to mark student papers in our large closet with the door shut. Maria didn't like the name Charlie; she liked to call him either Charles or CM. "It's good executive training," she said. At Rider I hosted a radio talk show. I delivered lectures for a WFIL-TV series "Great Women in History."

My salary at Rider was low and I had too many students in my classes, so I accepted a position as associate professor at Ulster Community College in Kingston, New York. We rented the upper floor of a two family house owned by a realtor. The lower floor apartment was rented to Frances and Bob Tigue, who worked for IBM. They had a daughter, Marissa, who became CM's playmate. Frances and Bob were a conservative couple like us and we became good friends. Frances's parents were poor Italian Americans from Appalachia. Her father died of "lung disease."

Maria knew how to get the lowest price possible for items that were negotiable. In Kingston we bought a 1966 Plymouth Sport Fury from Bob Beaumont, Inc. It was white with a white vinyl roof and plenty of chrome inside and outside. The interior was gold and it had bucket seats. She bargained so successfully that the dealer said he couldn't afford to give her the floor mats. "Keep the car and the mats," she replied. He surrendered and we got the car, the mats included, for $3824.22.

The president of Ulster Community College treated the faculty members like naval recruits. (He had been an officer in the US Navy.) The president and the faculty had no interest in scholarship. I believed the students were receiving an inferior education. The students remembered me in their 1965 yearbook dedication as "the scholar." In Kingston I researched the career of John Vanderlyn, an American artist, and I wrote an article on his career which appeared in *The New-York Historical Society Quarterly*. In 1967 Maria and I left Kingston for Rochester, New York, where I was hired as associate professor of history. I remained at Rochester Institute of Technology until I retired in 1994, with the rank of full professor. By that time my son Charles and his wife Joan had a baby daughter named Toni and Maria and I helped to take care of her.

Being with my granddaughter made me feel young again and gave me the opportunity to test my knowledge of comic books, since Toni enjoyed playing superheroes games with me. I provided most of the narrative and she provided most of the action. Sometimes I was Batman and she was Robin. She decided that Robin could transform himself into a cat with super powers. My characters created problems for society and her characters had to solve those problems. The Moleman created tunnels that could swallow oceans and crumble cities but Robin always intervened in time to save mankind from disaster. My character Gaston was forty-five years old and still in kindergarten and wanted everyone in the world to learn only the Humpty Dumpty nursery rhyme. Robin patiently explained to Gaston on numerous occasions that individuals had to know more than this rhyme in order to function in our complex society. On one occasion the Incredible Hulk accidently kicked a star into the bowl of oatmeal ready to be eaten by Galactus and Robin had to explain to the great god that it was not done intentionally. Toni decided that the Incredible Hulk was Robin's father. Often Robin became a lawyer in order to defend his positions and actions in courts.

In 1973 Maria and I bought our first and only house, a Tudor built in 1928 in the Meadowbrook area of Brighton, a suburb of Rochester. George Eastman, the founder of Kodak, had decided years earlier to make housing affordable for Kodak employees.

With this in mind Eastman had established the Eastman Savings and Loan Corporation and the Realty Corporation. Land for housing had been made available north of Kodak Park and east of Rochester in an area known as Meadowbrook. This was an example of welfare capitalism popular in the United States in the 1920's. Our house was one of the first buildings erected in Meadowbrook. The Meadowbrook Association came into existence, a governing body serving the community. Many Kodak employees settled in Meadowbrook and some rose to important positions in the company. The community was mostly Protestant in its religious affiliation. Eventually non-Kodak residents became the majority homeowners in Meadowbrook. We were the first Italian Americans in the neighborhood. There was concern until residents learned that I was a professor at RIT. "We were relieved," one of our new neighbors told us, "that you were not connected with the Mafia."

At RIT I taught a course on the history of Italian Americans. Most of the Italian students taking the course had one parent, usually the mother, who was an Italian American. Yet they identified as Italian Americans. I had in my class a girl who was not of Italian heritage but had lived among Italian Americans all of her life and considered herself an Italian American in her cultural outlook. While they identified as Italian Americans, they knew little about their culture and were eager to learn. I had to make it clear to my students that their Italian American identity was an evolving identity and not something static or simply in the past lives of their families. Discovery of self is a daily phenomenon.

An African American student named Bruce identified with me

because I came from a ghetto community in New York City like he did and because I was brought up by grandparents like him. He made me discover the fact that many of us have more than one identity.

The National Technical Institute for the Deaf is a college on the RIT campus. I taught deaf and hard-of-hearing students in my course History of Social Discrimination. I discovered that the deaf have a culture, traditions and a language of their own. Like Italian Americans they have been victims of discrimination. Professor Robert Panara, a deaf Italian American, taught at NTID. He is a poet-scholar proud of his Italian and deaf cultures. Influenced by deaf culture, I wrote articles on Isabel Crawford, a deaf Baptist missionary who worked with the Kiowa Indians of Oklahoma.

In Rochester I did research on the history of American Baptists, including Italian American Baptists. During my research visits to the Baptist Home in Fairport, New York, I met one of the most significant women in the history of that denomination. In March 1982 I interviewed Dr. Martha Jane Gifford, who passed away shortly after I met her. Gifford was born in Hornby, New York, on August 25, 1886. Martha was the youngest of five children, the daughter of farmers. She was brought up a Methodist by her mother. After graduating from the North Side High School in Corning, New York, she enrolled in a teacher training school and after graduation taught in country schools. She converted to the Baptist denomination, attended Kalamazoo College, the American Baptist College and finally the Rush Medical College of the University of Chicago. In 1916 she was appointed a missionary-surgeon to Burma by the

Women's American Baptist Foreign Mission Society. She worked in a hospital that treated only women and children. She performed surgery, and treated patients with malaria, cholera, smallpox and dysentery. On occasion she was in charge of a leprosy home. Dr. Gifford noted in the interview: "I believe in thoroughness and exactness in medicine. Physicians must meet the needs of their patients and must put themselves in the place of patients. They must have sympathy for people as well as training in medicine." Martha was totally deaf at the time of the interview. She had an older sister at the Fairport Home who looked after her.

On June 28, 1982, I interviewed a ninety-four year old Italian American nun named Eligia Mussi. Sister Eligia was born in Auburn, New York. Her parents were immigrants from Verona and met with no discrimination from their German neighbors. Her brother Angelo, a Cornell graduate, was the architect of the Barge Canal. Sister Eligia taught at St. Lucy's parochial school in Rochester. Most of the Italian immigrants who attended St. Lucy's Church worked in the shoe, button and clothing factories in the city. "They were hard-working people who saved their money to send their children to school," she told me. Many of the boys and girls she taught went on to become lawyers, physicians, teachers, priests and nuns. The school didn't offer Italian to the students. Father Mario Catalano, the pastor of the church, told the nuns that the children could speak their dialects at home but in school they had to learn the English language. In the early years of the migration to Rochester the Abruzzesi and the Neapolitans lived on the west side of the Genesee River and the Sicilians congregated on the east side. Following World War Two a large number of Italians especially from Sicily came to Rochester to work in the clothing factories. The newcomers assimilated rapidly and sent their children to college in large numbers.

My childhood interests resurfaced during my professional career. My lifelong interest in the American West led me to write an article on Baptist Chapel Cars, churches on trains that traveled throughout the American West. A childhood fascination for comic books led me to write an article on Spider-Man, a popular comic-book superhero. I did short biographies of comic-book artists Jack Kirby and Bob Kane for the American National Biography Online. My continuing search for my ethnic identity has led me to write books and articles on the Italian Americans. It has encouraged me to study both French and Italian literature. I have discovered my roots in the writings of Maupassant, Pirandello, Verga, Sciascia and Camilleri.

I made my first trip to Italy in late May 1969. I was invited to deliver a paper on the Italian immigrants in the United States at a conference sponsored by the University of Florence. Since there were student demonstrations at the university, the conferees delivered their talks at the Palazzo Vecchio. It was an important moment in my life. I felt at home among the Italians of Italy. I felt I belonged to two countries.

While working at RIT, I communicated with Dr. Leonard Covello. He informed me that he was starting the American Italian Historical Association and he wanted me, "one of his boys," to come to the first meeting to be held in East Harlem. At the meeting Dr. Covello introduced me to the other professors present: Rudolph J. Vecoli, Frank Cordasco, Salvatore LaGumina, and Luciano J. Iorizzo. Father Silvano Tomasi, the director of the Center for Migration Studies and a future archbishop, was also present. Professor Iorizzo and I established a lasting friendship. Luciano was born on March 31, 1930 to John Iorizzo and Adolorata Veneziale in Brooklyn. Following his mother's death shortly after his birth, Luciano lived an unsettled childhood going back and forth from his grandmother to his aunts and uncles. He found stability after his marriage to Martha Marilee Bridges in 1952. Marilee not only captivated Luciano, she also won over his family "big time." Luciano began his college teaching career at SUNY at Oswego in 1962, the year he won a Fulbright Scholarship. He earned his Ph.D. from Syracuse University. Professor Iorizzo had come a long way when I met him from his teenage years when he set pins at ten cents a line at a bowling establishment. In 1971 our book, *The Italian Americans*, was published by Twayne Publishers. A major theme of that study was the discrimination Italian Americans continued to confront in our times. We argued that a monolithic criminal conspiracy led by Italian Americans and called the Mafia was a myth.

We had never imagined that our book, a scholarly study, could be so controversial but it was. A journalist for the New York Times kept me on the phone for two hours hoping I would change my mind on the issue of crime among Italian Americans. I did not. Local television stations in Rochester picked up the story and announced that a professor was saying the American Mafia was a myth. Cliff Carpenter, a journalist for the Democrat and Chronicle, interviewed me and understood the bigotry Italian Americans were experiencing. In his column for March 26, 1971, he concluded, "It is a good book in that figuratively it takes us by the scruff of the neck and shakes us gently, demanding that we look at our fellow mortals more carefully and more sensitively."

A year earlier, at Columbus Circle in New York City a Unity Day rally was held attended by thousands of Italian Americans. Sponsored by the fledgling Italian American Civil Rights League and organized by Joseph Colombo, Sr., the reputed head of a crime family in New York, the celebrants heard speeches extolling the contributions made by Italian Americans to our country and speeches decrying the popular image of Italian Americans as a criminally-inclined people. Celebrants shouted "Italian is Beautiful" and "Italian Power." A year later, when our book appeared, the League leaders in New York City purchased copies in significant numbers to be placed in schools and libraries.

In 1971 in Rochester Chapter 21 of the Italian American Civil Rights League held its annual meeting at the Mapledale Party House. I was one of the guest speakers. Later, while I was talking with some of the leaders of the League, a young man asked Maria's friend, Mrs. LoCurto, to introduce him to "this gorgeous Italian woman." Mrs. LoCurto told him that Maria was happily married. "Peccato," the young man replied. Later, I asked Maria if she had found this man handsome. "Yes," she said, "but I don't believe in extramarital affairs."

Anthony Colombo, the son of Joseph Colombo, attended the

meeting at the Mapledale Party House. He had a bodyguard at his side. I told him I was proud to be an Italian American. He corrected me and said, "We are Italians not Italian Americans." Many businessmen were present, including my friend Joseph LoCurto who headed the fund-raising program to establish the Casa Italiana at Nazareth College. One of the speakers that evening was Frank Valenti, the most important racketeer in Rochester. He called for an end to discrimination against Italian Americans.

On November 3, 1970, the Democrat and Chronicle of Rochester printed statements that I made to one of its reporters on the subject of the Mafia myth in America. Replying to my contention that a monolithic Mafia conspiracy did not exist, Ralph Salerno, retired Superintendent of Detectives in the New York Police Department, was quoted as saying in the January 6, 1971 issue of the Democrat and Chronicle, "I believe it exists. I know it exists. I think there's sufficient intelligence that would convince any prudent man." Charles Siragusa, retired Federal Bureau of Narcotics agent, was reported to have responded to my contention with these remarks: "I've encountered this notion many, many times in my career. It comes from two types of people—gangsters themselves and unsuspecting people of good intentions." I replied that the concept of a sinister monolithic Mafia conspiracy was born in the 1880's and 1890's when many Americans blamed slums, tenement conditions, unemployment and criminal activities on immigrants and blacks. These were decades of intense nativism and racism. In the South, Italians as well as blacks were lynched. Let us fight crime and not Italian Americans, I concluded.

The social, economic and emotional price the Italian immigrants paid in America is a theme developed by Professor Rudolph J. Vecoli in an essay published in 1973: "This land was not hospitable to the Italians. Our hearts are not full of gratitude, because we know the price that was paid for that which we enjoy today, a price paid in sweat, tears, and blood; the cliché is nonetheless true. How many thousands of Italian immigrants were killed and mutilated in industrial accidents and mine disasters only God knows."[32]

My friend Louie Jap and I talked on the phone two years before he died. He was a businessman, had remarried after his divorce and had grandchildren. He was living in the Bronx. His mother Rose was still alive. She had supported three children and her husband, a petty bookie, by doing piecework in her home in East Harlem years ago. He told me my accent had changed. I didn't talk like someone who came from East Harlem. Many of the Braves had passed away. No Brave had become a gangster. Three of the Braves, Johnny Jew Boy, Georgie and Joey, had become cops.

In 1971, my grandmother was living with my mother in Hempstead. Grandpa had passed away at age eighty. My mother read *The Italian Americans* to my grandmother. My mother had to translate the chapters from English to the dialect of the immigrants from San Fratello, a dialect no longer spoken by the inhabitants of that village. My grandmother approved. She must have felt that she had contributed to this book. She had.

FRANK

It was a warm July day in 1981 in Brooklyn and Frank Faragasso, a friend of Maria's father, was reading his newspaper on his back porch. I waved to him from the porch of my mother-in-law's house and he came over to say hello. He told me he was depressed by the death of so many of his friends, including Joe Rampello. I asked him if he would like to talk about the "old days" in Brooklyn and this is the interview he gave me on that Summer day on my mother-in-law's porch:

Frank Faragasso was born under the Brooklyn Bridge in 1906. He was born in a Calabrese neighborhood, bordering on a Polish immigrant community. The Poles, a hard working people, hauled logs from the river while the Italians ran small businesses.

His father, Salvatore Faragasso, migrated from the town of Acri in Calabria to the Brooklyn Bridge area in 1900. Frank remembered that the Polish and Italian kids engaged in stone throwing fights. The Calabrese men belonged to the St. Angelo Society. The leaders of the society helped get jobs for the members. Once a year, on October 30th, the Calabresi celebrated the feast day honoring their patron saint.

Salvatore opened a small grocery store in the Brooklyn Bridge neighborhood. He bought his provisions from farmers and others at the Walloubout Market and was always on the alert for news of jobs for his friends. Salvatore was a sergeant major in Italy. He courted Louisa Rosa of Acri, talking to her behind a fence fifty feet from her house. Louisa grew up in a family of butchers. As a child she learned to cut meat for shepherds and others who took their animals to her family to be slaughtered, giving the Rosa family portions of the meat in a barter system. Louisa and Salvatore got married in 1900. He came to Brooklyn first and she followed two years later. Louisa ran the meat department in her husband's store. The store was located at York and Main streets. Salvatore and Louisa had eight children but only five survived infancy.

Frank grew up by the docks. He couldn't go to school because his earnings were needed to support the family. He delivered meat for his uncle who owned a butcher shop. By 1918 jobs were available for boys since the young men went off to war. At that time Frank got a job as a "galley boy" for Pulitzer's New York World. Working for ten dollars a week he assisted the printers who taught him how to run the presses. He worked for the World for thirteen years. Frank worked from six p.m. until three in the morning. On payday the printers pinned his ten-dollar bill inside his shirt, hiding his earnings from possible thieves as he walked home. His mother gave him twenty-five cents of the ten dollars. With this money he bought two hamburgers, a frank, a piece of pie and a cup of coffee. He ate this meal at Max's Busy Bee in the Bowery, a popular eatery for the Bowery's bums, where they could buy a hamburger for three cents. On Sundays he had six cents to spend, three for the movies and three for candy.

When the World closed during the Great Depression, Frank went to work for the Daily News, working on the presses for thirteen dollars a week. In 1927 he married Gertrude Serrantino. They had five children. His wife never worked. It was a matter of pride for working men to keep their wives at home. His lack of education deprived him of better jobs. Since he could never become a reporter, he moved up at the Daily News from menial jobs to eventually fixing and repairing machines.

Gertrude's father, Giacomo Serrantino, owned a bakery first at Fifth Avenue and Garfield, later on Union Street and finally on Navy Street. He was an immigrant from Naples. He delivered bread with his horse and wagon to Italian families in his neighborhood. Many bought on credit and never repaid him. Among the delinquent accounts were the families of racketeers. Even they were too poor to pay their bills to Giacomo.

Frank knew Ed Sullivan, a leading columnist for the Daily News. Frank needed a second job to make ends meet and asked Sullivan if he was aware of any job opportunities for him. Sullivan told Frank that he could get him a job in the kitchen at the Stork Club or at Radio City Music Hall. Frank liked the possibility of working at the Radio City Music Hall. Sullivan made an appointment for Frank to meet his friend Gus Eisell, the owner of the theater. Frank worked as a house detective, looking out for pickpockets and peeping toms who often bothered women in the powder room. He also ejected men who maliciously made noises and gestures intended to interrupt the dancing patterns of the Rockettes. He held this second job for one year.

In the early years of Prohibition Frank made extra money, thirty-five dollars a night, unloading liquor for Joe Adonis, who smuggled booze from Canada into New York City. Adonis had motorcycle cops guarding the smuggled liquor. Adonis was born Giuseppe Antonio Doto in Montemarano, a village near Naples. In 1915 he entered the United States illegally. He settled in Brooklyn, where he met Lucky Luciano. Adonis rose in the underworld after Luciano eliminated his competitors, Joe Masseria and Salvatore Maranzano. Adonis was one of four gunmen who killed Masseria in a Coney Island restaurant. At the peak of his career in the rackets Adonis had important interests in legal and illegal enterprises in Brooklyn. In 1953 he was deported to Italy. He lived the life of a signore in his villa near Naples until his death of a heart attack in 1972. In the 1920's Frank Faragasso opened a speakeasy in the Bedford-Stuyvesant section of Brooklyn, a tough neighborhood. He employed a Black singer, Delia Jackson, and a Black pianist-singer, Al Williams. Frank hired people to run his speakeasy. Frank's speakeasy was attracting large crowds and he was "in the money." Located at Utica Avenue and Schenectady Street, men drank, talked, played cards and "made out with the women." Frank made his own liquor. There was a police station at the corner but the cops never bothered him. The mobsters did. Mobsters opened a speakeasy across the street from Frank's and decided to put him out of business. One day nine mobsters entered his speakeasy. They tied him up, put an automatic to his head and destroyed his establishment. They may have been connected with the Luciano organization.

Later, Frank opened a saloon on Atlantic Avenue. The saloon also served as the Democratic Party Club in the neighborhood.

Men played cards and drank. Politicians came to the saloon to seek out voters. He operated the saloon for four years. Since he continued to hold his job at the Daily News, he employed people to manage his speakeasy and later his saloon. After the saloon folded, he bought a taxi cab for $5,000.

Frank held his job at the Daily News from 1930 to 1960, when he found employment as a security guard at Brooklyn College, only a few blocks from his home.

Maria brought us some lemonade and cookies. We talked some more and then he went back to his porch to finish reading his paper. That was the last time I saw Frank Faragasso.

FATHER JOSEPH

I arrived at the rectory about noon on April 26, 1979. A woman greeted me and offered me some lemonade. I waited for Father Joseph Beatini in a comfortable room on the second floor. The woman reappeared fifteen minutes later and told me that "Father B. couldn't climb stairs since he had been ill recently." I went downstairs to greet him. He introduced me to his assistant pastor, Daniel V. Hogan. Father Beatini was a tall man who was never able to control his weight. At the time of our meeting he was pastor of Assumption of Our Lady Church in Fairport, New York. He had spent the morning attending a charity fashion show sponsored by the women of his parish. Father Beatini had modeled several jackets at the event. His cook prepared lunch for the three of us with Father Beatini giving her instructions in Italian as well as English, hoping that over time she would learn a few phrases in Italian. At 1:10 Father Beatini and I went to his study. He insisted that I sit at his desk since I would be taking notes during the interview. What follows is my transcript of our conversation on that sunny cool day in Western New York.

Joseph Beatini was born in Seneca Falls, New York on December 15, 1921. His parents, Carlo and Annunciata, were immigrants from Licciana Nardi in Tuscany. Carlo arrived in Seneca Falls in 1899 and Annunciata came six years later. Joseph was the youngest of fourteen children, nine dying at birth or in their infancy. Carlo, a shoemaker, decided to work at Gould's Pumps, where he made a respectable living.

Charles Fornesi, Joseph's great-uncle on Annunciata's side, was the first member of the family to come to New York. Fornesi settled in Syracuse first, but when salesmen told him about opportunities in Seneca Falls, he decided to go there. Fornesi, the first Italian to settle in Seneca Falls, encouraged friends and relatives from Licciana Nardi to join him there. Many came. Fornesi ran a grocery store and a bank for the new arrivals from Italy.

Before the arrival of many immigrants from Licciana Nardi, few Italians lived in Seneca Falls and Carlo and Annunciata learned English quickly in order to communicate with their neighbors. Annuciata, a bright woman, had attended school in Italy. Joseph's aunt came when there were many Italians in Seneca Falls and she spoke English with difficulty.

Annunciata liked to say that she was treated like a lady in Italy but in Seneca Falls she worked long hours, raising her children and taking in Italian boarders to make ends meet. They lived on Center Street, located on the South Side of the town. The Tuscans occupied that area in the early years of settlement.

Benny Colella, a Neapolitan, found himself one day by mistake in Seneca Falls. He noted how prosperous the Tuscans were in the town and decided to settle there and encourage Italians from five towns near Naples to join him. Many came and established the community called Rumseyville. Tuscans and Neapolitans remained segregated from each other at first. Integration came by the second generation.

The Beatini family attended St. Patrick's Roman Catholic Church, once an Irish church. Joseph enjoyed his childhood and played with twenty kids in his neighborhood. He went to St. Patrick's parochial school and encountered no discrimination. His older brother did. Joseph's family was very close and they spent time visiting other Italian families. The mutual benefit society established by the Tuscans was devoted primarily to planning and participating in family events. There was a large field in back of the society's headquarters and the kids played there often. One game was throwing a cheese mold. The kid who threw it the farthest won a prize.

All the kids learned Italian in high school from Frances D'Urso. Joseph spoke a Tuscan dialect that was close to Italian and he learned Italian with no difficulty. When he entered the seminary his mother died. His father had passed away earlier. In 1949 Joseph Beatini, now an ordained priest, was sent to St. Francis of Assisi Church in Auburn, New York. He remained there for five years, delivering the sermons in Italian. In 1954 he was transferred to St. Francis Xavier Church on Bay Street in Rochester, New York. He remained there until 1970.

A new wave of Italian immigrants came to work in the clothing factories in Rochester after the Second World War. Many were Sicilians from the town of Valguarnera. They were literate and Italian-speaking Italians. "These were days when I thought I was in Rome," Father Beatini told me. It was a long interview and we were both tired. We decided to have a second meeting to finish the story. We met again on May 30th at the same place.

The tailor factories in Rochester needed workers in the 1950's and representatives of the factories went to Sicily to recruit them. Meanwhile, the earlier immigrants in Rochester sent word back to Valguarnera that opportunities existed for clothing workers. Many came. Italian immigrants made up five thousand members of Beatini's church on Bay Street.

Father Beatini needed baptismal and other records of the immigrants and began a correspondence with Giacomo Magno, pastor of St. Christopher's Church in Valguarnera. Soon, friendly letters were being exchanged. Immigrants wrote to Father Magno, telling him how pleased they were with the work of Father Beatini. Magno was relieved that their faith was in good hands and told Beatini how delighted he was with him when he visited Valguarnera in 1968. Upon the death of Magno, Father Giarizzo, a young priest, became pastor of St. Christopher's. He visited Rochester four times in the sixties and heard confessions. "We put him to work," Father Beatini told me. The immigrants gave him money for the renovation of St. Christopher's and St. Francis's churches in Valguarnera.

Ferdinand LaDelfa and his wife were immigrants from Valguarnera and Ferdinand became a close friend to Beatini. Ferdinand had left his son Reno to continue his medical education in Catania. Reno visited his parents in the summer months and became an admirer of Beatini. He decided that he wanted to become a priest but didn't want to show disrespect for his father. "His father hit the ceiling when he heard that Reno wanted to be a priest," Beatini said. Beatini managed to reconcile father and son and at the time of the interview Reno was finishing his second year at St. Bernard's Seminary in Rochester.

"Get into the American way of life," Beatini told the immigrants. He encouraged them to participate in all parish programs and didn't set aside special programs for them. Since they had Bible study classes in Sicily, he continued these studies in Rochester. Study groups were conducted in Italian. "If you need the Italian language," he told them, "it is there, but get into the American way of life. Don't give up the Italian language and heritage, but learn English."

The Valguarnesi attended three Catholic churches in Rochester: Holy Redeemer, St. Michael's and St. Francis Xavier. The tailor factories where they worked were located near these churches. The newcomers didn't have cars and bought houses near the factories and churches. Mt. Carmel had many earlier arriving Italian Americans but it wasn't located near the factories; the newcomers did not worship there.

The earlier arriving Italian Americans of Rochester believed the newcomers had it easy because they came in a period of prosperity while they had to suffer hardships during the Great Depression. When the new immigrants came, Beatini noted, "they were already on third base." Within a short period of time, they bought houses in the suburbs and sent their children to college.

Beatini believes that the greatest contribution made by the Italians to America was their strong concept of family. His assistant pastor in Fairport is not Italian but he feels most comfortable in Italian homes with Italian families.

Father Beatini has an award hanging on a wall in his small study, an award given to him by the Italian Republic for his service to Italian immigrants. Nothing could please him more he confessed to me at the conclusion of the interview.[33]

KATHERINE

Catarina Zimbalatti was born in New York City on November 6, 1917. She was the first of two daughters of Vincent Zimbalatti, an immigrant from Reggio Calabria, and Sarah DiGregorio, a native New Yorker. Vincent worked as a candy maker for the Joyva company, rising to the position of foreman. His recipes were used in the making of the company's candies. He was a devoted father and husband and had many friends. Vincent passed away in 1973. Sarah was an "immaculate" homemaker and the "master" of her household. The second of seven children, she was a second mother to her brothers and sisters always looking out for their best interests. Often she helped neighborhood mothers take care of their sick children. She died in her forties.

The family moved when Catarina was six years old from 340 East Sixth Street between First and Second avenues to West Street in the Gravesend section of Brooklyn. From urban Manhattan the family now lived in a rural neighborhood. Tony Bennett and his family lived in Astoria and were related through marriage to Catarina's family. The two families would get together often for Sunday dinner. Tony's brother was taking singing lessons but Tony was the better singer. Catarina was impressed with the voice of the future legendary popular entertainer.

Catarina was a bright student. She attended P.S.216, P.S.95 and Lincoln High School where she completed her education. In elementary school the teachers called her Katherine and the name change stuck. An attractive, intelligent, poised brunette with a high school diploma and secretarial skills, Katherine was hired as the boss's secretary at Mullen's, a furniture store in Brooklyn. An efficient secretary she held an important position with the company. Katherine says she was "a big shot."

Rosie Crapanzano and her brother Joseph worked for Mullen's but they were not "big shots." Joseph worked in the mailroom. Katherine thought he was "cute" but only a "kid" with a dead end job. Joseph was attracted to Katherine but he was too shy to ask her for a date. He sent his brother Ralph, a dental student, to speak on his behalf. Katherine took her time making up her mind regarding Joseph but finally agreed to date him. She was pleased that Joseph was ambitious and was taking accounting classes at Pace College. But it took a courtship of ten years to convince Katherine to marry him.

Joseph Crapanzano was born on April 14, 1920 in Brooklyn, New York. He was a handsome young man who looked like Robert Taylor, a movie star. As a husband and father he was a good provider, rising to the position of director of purchasing at Blue Cross. He played an important role in getting a job at Blue Cross for Maria Rampello, his favorite niece. When Maria and I were ready to leave Brooklyn for Trenton, New Jersey, he got us a good deal for our first car, a Falcon, from an auto dealer he knew in Manhattan. When he learned that Maria needed a typewriter, he carried a huge typewriter on the subway from Manhattan to Brooklyn for her.

Katherine and Joseph had two children, Peter, a dentist, and Anita, the director of personnel at Empire BlueCross BlueShield and a licensed teacher. Anita remembers her father as a playful "free spirit." As a child he taught her "how to dance on his feet" and to "sample" wholesome pleasures and entertainments. He enjoyed taking her to Coney Island on

Summer Tuesdays where they watched the fireworks while munching on popcorn. An avid sports fan, he took his daughter to many sporting events held at Madison Square Garden. When Anita was ten years old, he took her to see her first Broadway show. They dined in an "elegant" restaurant in Greenwich Village. He encouraged Anita to try dishes Katherine, an excellent cook, did not prepare at home.

After her marriage, Katherine left work to become a homemaker, looking after her family, including her father, a widower. She insisted that her children excel in school. When she came with her family to the "Big House" on Bedford Avenue, she was always enveloped in the aromas of the dishes she had prepared for us. Katherine learned the cultures and traditions of her Irish and Jewish neighbors and often cooked traditional ethnic dishes. Of course, her meals were sumptuous affairs. Family gatherings at the "Big House" were attended by Joseph and Katherine Crapanzano and their children "Little" Peter and Anita, Vincent and Helen Crapanzano and their children "Big" Peter and Toni, Ralph and Janet Crapanzano and their daughters Susan and Vivian, Rosie and Joseph Dragonetti and their daughter Lisa, Salvatore and Maria Mondello and our son Charles and other relatives and friends on occasion. Our hosts were the owners of the "Big House": Joseph and Lena Rampello, "Old" Aunt Rose and Uncle Ralph Crapanzano, Vivian and Victor Faro, and Peter and Antonina Crapanzano. Gatherings were held in the cellar or the back yard. The women insisted on doing all the cooking for cellar events while the cookouts were controlled by the men. Cookouts featured franks and hamburgers while cellar events usually featured meatballs and pasta, chicken, sausages and fish. Wine and pastries were served too. Grandpa Peter was so careful peeling his apples that the skins resembled coils when he was finished. After the cellar meals the men played cards and the women talked. I remember Cousin Vinnie Parisi playing his accordian for our enjoyment once or twice. Occasionally the women huddled to hear one of Old Aunt Rose's racy stories. The men were not allowed to hear these stories. All we heard was the laughter at the end of each. I learned years later that when Old Aunt Rose talked about "ricotta" she was not talking about cheese. Joe Dragonetti would sneak out of the cellar after eating and enjoy the company of the television set in an upstairs room. He followed sporting events on television especially the Dodgers and later the Mets games. On a few occasions Anita and her father came later after a ball game. Lena felt Maria and I were too quiet at these functions.

Tragedy came on June 23, 1973, when Joseph died of a sudden heart attack. This devastating blow tested Katherine's indomitable will. Katherine and Anita wanted Peter to continue his studies in dental school. The women had to shoulder the family's financial responsibilities. Katherine went to her priest at Our Lady of Grace to see if he could help her find employment. He made an appointment for her to see Father Joseph M. Sullivan, head of Catholic Charities in the Diocese of Brooklyn. The future bishop hired her as his secretary. Katherine describes Bishop Sullivan as a brilliant writer and "terrific" administrator. Katherine continued to remain an active parishioner at Our Lady of Grace, participating in many of the societies.

On September 11, 2001 Anita got to work early as usual at her office on the twenty-ninth floor of the North Tower of the World Trade Center. She and the members of her staff felt the building sway and heard a "deep" sound. A short time later a woman ran into their department screaming hysterically that the elevators were falling. Not knowing that terrorists had smashed a jetliner into the building, Anita and the others assumed a helicopter had hit the tower. There was no announcement. "We have to get out of here," Anita told the members of her department. They didn't panic. As they were going down the stairs, firemen passed them running up. Anita saw the paraplegic who worked for her company on the twenty-seventh floor. He assured her someone was coming to help him get out of the building. Stairwells were filling up with water as Anita neared the exit. There was a terrible smell. It was the smell of jet fuel but Anita didn't know this.

"Sal, come here quick," shouted Maria from the living room. "The World Trade Center has just been hit by two jetliners." We stared at the television screen in disbelief. "Did Anita go to work today?" Maria asked. "Does she work at the World Trade Center?" I replied. "I don't know," she said.

Anita and her friend Denise began running after clearing the building. Debris was falling but didn't hit the two women. Onlookers were saying that a jetliner had crashed into the building. Denise wanted to stop to smoke a cigarette. "This is no time for that," Anita said. "We have to get out of here."

"I'm trying to get Aunt Katherine on the phone," Maria told me. "She must be at work in Brooklyn."

Anita and Denise kept running North. They were covered with soot. When the second tower fell they stopped and cried. They reached Central Park. People were enjoying the day. Some were walking their dogs. Strollers were unaware of the inferno downtown.

Peter called the World Trade Center but only got a recording telling him to leave a message. Anita's friend Romolo was in Rome and was frantic. Katherine was not aware of her daughter's narrow escape.

Anita finally reached a friend's apartment. He took Denise home by car and drove Anita to fetch Katherine in Brooklyn. Anita made it back home at eleven o'clock.

She got Romolo's daughter on the phone in Rome. "I'm okay," Anita told her. "Thank God. Romolo is going insane."

The paraplegic died at Ground Zero.

Now in her late eighties Katherine lives with Anita in central New Jersey near Peter and his wife Betty and their son Adam. Katherine and Anita call Adam "their prince." She commands a very alert mind but the years have slowed her physically. Katherine values her family above all else. She exemplifies the ideal Italian American mother honored among Italians and featured in American popular culture.[34]

SALVATORE

I met him at the "Big House" on Bedford Avenue. He was a distinguished man. An intellectual. He talked and looked like a college professor. He came often to visit his nephew Joseph Rampello.

Salvatore Rampello was born in Raffadali, Sicily on May 11, 1892 and died in Brooklyn, New York on Thanksgiving Day 1978. Salvatore, a redhead with gray-green eyes, was a militant Socialist in his native village and participated actively in a movement to win Sicily for the Italian Socialists. In Raffadali he was also known as a competent teacher and architect. He was an occasional barber. He became an active pacifist after his military service in World War I and cringed at the sight of blood after his war experience. Salvatore did not like to eat pasta with tomato sauce because the sauce was red. During the war he was wounded on three occasions and jailed once for insubordination. His mother, fearing that his political opponents might take his life in post-war Sicily, begged him to go to the United States, a country where she believed men were not harmed for holding passionate views on freedom and liberty. In October 1921 Salvatore arrived in New York City. He eventually opened a barbershop on Avenue U and Coney Island Avenue. On January 27, 1927 he married Mary DeLuca at St. Gregory's Roman Catholic Church in Brooklyn. They had three children: Joseph, Maria and Thomas.

While courting Mary DeLuca, Salvatore wrote her love letters. He called Mary "divine" and hoped their love would last "forever." She was a "radiant star" and the "queen of my heart." She was his "goddess" and her eyes were so "brilliant" that they "hypnotize me." Salvatore wrote to Mary's parents asking for her hand in marriage. Mrs. DeLuca responded affirmatively and felt "honored" that Salvatore wished to marry Mary.

Mary DeLuca was born in Brooklyn and was much younger than Salvatore. Mary's parents, Marino DeLuca and Marina Lauricella, were born in Isola Salina, a small island near Sicily. The island's major product was the growing and packaging of capers. Marino and Marina migrated to Brooklyn in the late nineteenth century. They had four children, a boy and three girls. In the beginning they lived in a small dwelling, the front room serving as a grocery store. During the winter months when the East River was frozen, Marino would walk on the river itself to get to the Fulton Fish Market, where he bought fish and produce for his store.

Salvatore Rampello made a comfortable living as a barber and found it possible to rent houses for his family that were architecturally interesting to his tastes. The family lived at 1715 Avenue T, a residence built by an artist. It had tiled ceilings and stain-glass windows. Later, they moved to another beautiful home on East Thirty-eighth Street and Avenue S.

After work Salvatore devoted time to his manuscript, a guidebook for the human race that was written in Italian and never submitted to a publisher. It examined current events, the consequences of industrial and technological changes upon humanity and numerous other subjects. He predicted the importance of credit cards in modern times. Indeed, a fertile mind. "When Daddy was sitting at his desk writing, we all had to be quiet," his daughter remembers.[35]

In his manuscript Salvatore speculated on the meaning of liberty, a concept he held so dearly that he was forced to leave Sicily for defending it in his public speeches. Salvatore Rampello believed that in modern times man, the "author of society," had become the "product of society." However, society at present could not guarantee that men would live in peace with justice and liberty. Liberty had become an arbitrary concept without rights and duties. True liberty, Salvatore believed, could be a reality when the rights of each did not threaten the rights of everyone else. But this concept of liberty could not triumph because the prevailing view defined liberty as the right of each individual to do all in his power to assure his own comfort. Liberty was not possible under modern dictatorial or democratic governments. A revolution was needed to create a truly free government, a government that would guarantee "a technocratic direction" to assure us all of an annual living income sufficient to keep up with the cost of living. Only in this way can people live in liberty with peace and justice in a "universal brotherhood." When he wrote on liberty he appeared to blend American and Sicilian views.

Salvatore identified with the poetry of Mario Rapisardi, born in Catania, Sicily in 1844. He was especially impressed with Rapisardi's masterpiece Giobbe; the protagonist in this poem became a symbol of suffering humanity in Rapisardi's generation. Rapisardi died in Catania in 1912, one of the most celebrated poets in modern Italian history.

In his manuscript Salvatore expressed his strong opposition to American foreign policy. American military action in Southeast Asia was not needed since the countries in that region did not threaten vital U.S. interests. The United States and Israel were depriving the Palestinians of their homeland. NATO, an alliance stemming from the Cold War, prevented Western Europe from forming a counterbalance to the pernicious U.S. influences worldwide. To successfully fight poverty throughout the world, warfare had to be abolished. A universal language would help to mitigate world problems.

Salvatore was a student of the International Monetary Fund established at Bretton Woods, New Hampshire. In his "Leadership Universale" sections of his manuscript he had long advocated monetary reform. Unfortunately, the Nixon Administration initiative in the Jamaica agreement was another example of "palliatives and expedients." In his manuscript he gave a detailed account of his reasons for disappointment.

Salvatore was fascinated by the geological changes on the earth over time and believed that change and diversity were also characteristic of our political, economic, cultural and social lives as humans on this ever shifting planet. We had to accept the fact that political "isms" would appear in each generation often in conflict with one another.

He spent happy hours with his wife and children, teaching them to appreciate and enjoy the cultures of New York City and the blessings of American society. He especially enjoyed taking them to beaches, the Brooklyn Museum of Art and Prospect Park. He took them to see countless movies at the Mayfair Theater, a movie house across the street from his barbershop. He read to them at home and he sang Italian arias with his daughter while they were cleaning dishes after meals. However, he believed the entertainment media, movies included, were wrong in their depictions of the influence of Sicilian mafiosi.

The campaigns conducted against the Mafia in Italy and the United States were smoke screens, Salvatore argued, allowing corrupt government officials and racketeers to pursue their criminal activities with impunity. In both countries Sicilians were made the scapegoats and their culture was denigrated. Problems in society did not stem from the Mafia. Corrupt government officials in top positions were far more responsible than mafiosi for the social ills of nations. "In fatti si dice—che il pesce quando puzza—il suo fetore comincia dalla testa e—non mica dalla coda!" (In fact it is said that when the fish is putrid the stink begins from the head not from the tail.) Capitalists had failed to solve the manifold problems stemming from poverty and a program based on socialistic solutions was imperative.

"He was interested in the world around us," his daughter told me recently, "and taught us to appreciate it. He was a loving father and wanted to share with us what he loved and enjoyed." He was also a social reformer whose views never reached the public. A silent revolutionary cutting hair for a living and confiding his views to my father-in-law.

Joseph, Salvatore's oldest child, became a businessman. Even after he was diagnosed with multiple sclerosis he continued his graduate studies and received his MBA. Thomas became a company mechanic. Maria decided not to attend college. "I wanted to be a member of the world," she told me recently. The women she knew who had graduated from college were wrapped up in themselves and had little interest in learning about the world around them. Like her father she enjoyed reading and learning as continuing experiences. She worked with the deaf and blind at the Industrial Home for the Blind in Brooklyn. She learned sign language. She did recordings for the blind. Later, Maria took a job as receptionist and secretary at St. Vincents Foster Care Home in Brooklyn. Before seeing the psychiatrist the children were treated to refreshments by Maria and played games with her. Maria built a doll house for the children and they were allowed to play with it. Maria became upset when she discovered that there was only one doll for the five children in their foster home, so she bought them each a doll with her own money. The children responded by giving Maria a surprise "thank you party." Her mother, a pleasant woman, had served as "an audience" for her father's ideas. Maria made successful efforts to put some of her father's ideas concerning assistance to the poor and needy into practice. Salvatore influenced his family if not the reading public in Italy.

NOTES

1. Edwin Fenton. *Immigrants and Unions, A Case Study: Italians and American Labor, 1870–1920.* New York: Arno Press 1975. pp. 209–219. – "Some Special Health Problems of Italians in New York City: A Preliminary Survey." Reprinted from the Quarterly Bulletin, New York City Department of Health, Vol. II, No. 3, 1934. In *Italians in the City: Health and Related Social Needs,* Arno Press 1975. – Robert F. Foerster. *The Italian Emigration of Our Times.* New York: Russell & Russell. 1968. p. 333.
2. Salvatore Mondello. *The Italian Immigrant in Urban America, 1880–1920, as Reported in the Contemporary Periodical Press.* New York: The Arno Press. 1980. p. 142. – Henry Adams to Charles Francis Adams, Jr. June 9, 1860 in *The Letters of Henry Adams,* Volume One, 1858–1868. Cambridge, Massachusetts: Belknap Press of Harvard University Press, 1982, pp. 162–172.
3. Baryd Still. *Mirror for Gotham.* New York: New York University Press. 1956. pp. 281–2.
4. Giovanni Verga. *Tutte le Novelle.* Milano: Oscar Mondadori. 1980. Volume 1, pp. 37–59.
5. Verga. pp. 186–199.
6. On the subject of Italian Fascism, see R. J. B. Bosworth. *Mussolini.* New York: Oxford University Press. 2002. – Renzo DeFelice. *Breve Storia del Fascismo.* Milano: Oscar Mondadori. 2002. – Ignazio Silone. *Il Fascismo: Origini e Sviluppo.* Milano: Oscar Mondadori. 2003. – Philip V. Cannistraro. "Pope, Generoso." American National Biography Online. Oxford University Press. Feb. 2000.
7. Emma Alaimo. *Proverbi Siciliani.* Firenze: Giunti-Martello. 1974.
8. Caroline Singer. "An Italian Saturday." The Century (March 1921), pp. 591–600.
9. Rose Basile Green. *Primo Vino.* South Brunswick and New York: A. S. Barnes. 1974, p. 37.
10. Malachy Carroll and Pol deLeon Albaret. *Three Studies in Simplicity: Padre Pio. Martin dePorres, Benedict the Black.* Chicago: Franciscan Herald Press. 1974.
11. Michael Seidel. Streak: *Joe DiMaggio and the Summer of '41.* New York: Penguin Books. 1989.
12. William A. Borst. "Lombardi, Ernesto Natali". American National Biography Online, Feb. 2000.

13. Anonimo. *I Tre Minchioni di Palermo*. Siracusa: Nando Russo Editore. 1983. p. 90.
14. Ibid., p. 84.
15. Luigi Vasi. *Delle Origini e Vicende di San Fratello*. Palermo: Stabilimento Tipografico Virzi. 1882. p. 52.
16. Giuseppe Bonaviri. *Fiabe Siciliane*. Milano: Oscar Mondadori. 1990. pp. 115–116 and 119–121.
17. Leonardo Sciascia. *La Corda Pazza: Scrittori e Cose della Sicilia*. Milano: Adelphi Edizioni. 1984. pp. 209–210.
18. Leonard Covello. *The Heart Is the Teacher*. New York: McGraw-Hill. 1958, pp. 31–35. – Anna C. Ruddy. *The Heart of the Stranger: The Story of Little Italy*. New York: reprint of the Arno Press. 1975. – *Protestant Evangelism among Italians in America*. New York: reprint of the Arno Press. 1975, pp. 149–151.
19. David R. Bewley-Taylor. "Costello, Frank". American National Biography Online. Oxford University Press. Feb. 2000. – Leonard Katz. *Uncle Frank: The Biography of Frank Costello*. New York: Drake Publishers. 1973.
20. Alessio DiGiovanni. *Lu Saracinu*. Palermo: Edizioni "il Vespro" s.p. A. 1980.
21. Leonardo Sciascia. *La Sicilia Come Metafora*. Milano: Arnoldo Mondadori Editore. 1979. pp. 35–61.
22. Andrea Camilleri. *Storie di Montalbano*. Milano: Arnoldo Mondadori Editore. 2002. – Lawrence Durrell. *Sicilian Carousel*. New York: The Viking Press. 1977, pp. 61–106. – Santi Correnti. *Storia e Folklore di Sicilia*. Milano: Mursia. 1973. p. 83.
23. Francesco Cordasco. "Covello, Leonard". American National Biography Online. Oxford University Press. Feb. 2000. – For the work of Dolci see Jerre Mangione. *A Passion for Sicilians: The World Around Danilo Dolci*. New York: William Morrow. 1968. – Joseph G. Fucilla. *The Teaching of Italian in the United States: A Documentary History*. New Brunswick, New Jersey: American Association of Teachers of Italian. 1967. Reprint Edition 1975 by the Arno Press. pp. 262–277. – Leonard Covello. *The Social Background of the Italo-American School Child*. Leiden: E. J. Brill. 1967. pp. 416–448.
24. Thomas Kessner. "LaGuardia, Fiorello Henry". American National Biography Online. Oxford University Press. Feb. 2000.
25. David M. Esposito. "Marcantonio, Vito Anthony". American National Biography Online. Oxford University Press. Feb. 2000.
26. Felice A. Bonadio. "Corsi, Edward". American National Biography

Online. Oxford University Press. Feb. 2000.

27. Barbara L. Ciccarrelli. "Giannini, Attilio Henry". American National Biography Online. Oxford University Press. Feb. 2000.

28. Tony Thomas. "Warren, Harry". American National Biography Online. Feb. 2000.

29. Stephen G. Marshall. "Capra, Frank". American National Biography Online. Oxford University Press. Feb. 2000. – Frank Capra. *The Name Above the Title: An Autobiography*. New York: Random House. 1971.

30. Harold Seymour. Baseball: *The Golden Age*. New York: Oxford University Press. 1971. pp. 457–460.

31. William L. Riordon. *Plunkitt of Tammany Hall*. New York: E. P. Dutton. 1963.

32. Rudolph J. Vecoli. "Born Italian: Color Me Red, White, and Green." Soundings. Spring 1973, pp. 117–123.

33. Salvatore Mondello. "The Italians," in James S. Pula, ed. *Ethnic Rochester*. Lanham, MD: University of America Press. 1985. – Jerre Mangione. *Mount Allegro: A Memoir of Italian American Life*. New York: Columbia University Press. 1981.

34. Interview with Katherine and Anita Crapanzano, conducted on March 30, 2005

35. Interview with Maria Rampello, conducted on April 2, 2005. – Salvatore Rampello. "Leadership Internazionale: Nuovo Ordine." He began writing his book in January 1970 and completed it on July 4, 1974.

A Bibliographical Note

For additional readings on the Italian Americans see the extensive bibliography in Jerre Mangione and Ben Morreale. *La Storia: Five Centuries of the Italian American Experience*. New York: Harper-Collins Publishers. 1992. Another extensive bibliography is found in Luciano J. Iorizzo and Salvatore Mondello. *The Italian Americans*. Revised Edition. New York: Twayne Publishers. 1980. These two books are general histories of the Italian Americans. Two additional general histories are the following: Alexander DeConde. *Half Bitter, Half Sweet. An Excursion into Italian-American History*. New York: Charles Scribner's Sons. 1971 and Erik Amfitheatrof. *The Children of Columbus: An Informal History of the Italians in the New World*. Boston: Little, Brown and Company. 1973.

An award-winning book on the subject of discrimination against Italian Americans is Thomas A. Guglielmo. *White on Arrival: Italians, Race, Color and Power in Chicago, 1890–1945*. New York: Oxford University Press. 2003.

On Italian East Harlem see Leonard Covello. *The Heart Is the Teacher*. New York: McGraw-Hill. 1958 and Robert Anthony Orsi. *The Madonna of 115th Street: Faith and Community in Italian Harlem, 1880–1950*. New Haven: Yale University Press. 1985.

For readers of Italian I recommend the following books on Sicilian culture and society:
Giuseppe Bonaviri. *Fiabe Siciliane*. Milano: Oscar Mondadori. 1990.
Andrea Camilleri. *Storie di Montalbano*. Milano: I Meridiani, Arnoldo Mondadori. 2002.
Denis Mack Smith. *Storia della Sicilia Medievale e Moderna*. Bari: Editori Laterza. 1983.
Luigi Pirandello. *Tutto il Teatro in Dialetto*. Milano: Tascabili Bompiani. 1994.
Leonardo Sciascia. *La Corda Pazza: Scrittori e Cose della Sicilia*. Milano: Adelphi Edizioni. 1991.

Sciascia. *Il Giorno della Civetta*. Milano: Adelphi Edizioni. 1993.
Giovanni Verga. *Tutte le Novelle*. Milano: Oscar Mondadori. 1968.
(CD: Il Narratore. Audio Antologia della Letteratura Italiana.
Giovanni Verga: "La Lupa" e "Rosso Malpelo.")
Elio Vittorini. *Conversazione in Sicilia*. Torino: Einaudi Editore.
1981.
There are two books on San Fratello.
Luigi Vasi. *Delle Origini e Vicende di San Fratello*. Palermo:
Stabilimento Tipografico Virzi. 1882. ("L'Amata" is found on page
52.)
Benedetto Rubino. *Folklore di S. Fratello*. Palermo 1914.

Toots Mondello may be heard on CD: "Toots Mondello" VMP0111
Vintage Music Productions 2002. New Hamphire USA.

About the Author

Salvatore Mondello was born on February 27, 1932 in East Harlem, New York City. Brought up by Sicilian immigrant grandparents, he developed an early appreciation for Sicilian culture and traditions, an appreciation that shaped and defined his career and personality.

Equally significant was the cultural environment of Italian East Harlem, especially its street culture and its schools. He attended Benjamin Franklin High School, where he came under the influence of Dr. Leonard Covello, the celebrated principal of the school and the founder of the American Italian Historical Association. Covello and Dina DiPino, his Italian language teacher, taught him to value and enjoy his Italian roots while novelist Charles Calitri introduced him to the profound delights of American and English literature.

At NYU, where Mondello received his Ph.D. in history in 1960 he learned the importance of historical knowledge from Bayrd Still, Ray W. Irwin, Leo Gershoy and A. William Salomone. Unforgettable was the humanity of the Polish poet-scholar Ludwik Krzyzanowski.

Mondello taught history at Rider College, Ulster Community College and the Rochester Institute of Technology where he holds the title of Professor Emeritus. He has received awards from the State University of New York and the National Endowment for the Humanities.

He is the author of many scholarly articles and has three published books to his credit. *The Italian Americans* (Twayne Publishers, 1971) coauthored with Luciano J. Iorizzo, was a national best seller and the first scholarly treatment of that subject. It appeared in a revised edition in 1980. Mondello's doctoral dissertation, *The Italian Immigrant in Urban America, 1880–1920, as Reported in the Contemporary Periodical Press*, was published by the Arno Press of the New York Times in 1980. In 1989, the Edwin Mellen Press published Mondello's *The Private Papers of John Vanderlyn (1775–1852) American Portrait Painter*.

Married to the late Maria Rampello, Professor Mondello has a son and a granddaughter.

Printed in the United States
53176LVS00003B/499-558